Self and Identity: The Basics is a jargon-free and accessible introduction that draws on key theories and ideas in Social Psychology to explore the ways that other people affect our thoughts, feelings, and behaviours. Highlighting selfhood as a function of identity, the book shows that it is our relationships with others in our social world that largely determine who we are.

"Who am I?" It's a question that most all humans have grappled with at some point or another. This book seeks to answer this question through relatable examples that show how psychological theory can be applied to our own lives. It considers the philosophical and psychological context in which ideas about selfhood have developed and reviews the ways that the people around us, and the groups that we belong to, affect who we are. Finally, these ideas are considered in the context of real-world phenomena and behaviours; for instance, how we use language, conflict between groups, and social influence.

With a glossary of key terms, suggestions for further reading, and chapter summaries, this book is an ideal introduction for students of social psychology and related fields. It will be of interest to anyone who wants to gain social psychological insight into who they are and how others got them there.

Dr Megan E. Birney is a Senior Lecturer in Social Psychology and Individual Differences at Staffordshire University in the UK. Her research focuses on identity processes, intergroup relations, communication, stigma, obedience, conspiracy theories, and social exclusion.

The Basics Series

The Basics is a highly successful series of accessible guidebooks which provide an overview of the fundamental principles of a subject area in a jargon-free and undaunting format.

Intended for students approaching a subject for the first time, the books both introduce the essentials of a subject and provide an ideal springboard for further study. With over 50 titles spanning subjects from artificial intelligence (AI) to women's studies, *The Basics* is an ideal starting point for students seeking to understand a subject area.

Each text comes with recommendations for further study and gradually introduces the complexities and nuances within a subject.

SELF AND IDENTITY

THE BASICS

Megan E. Birney

Routledge
Taylor & Francis Group

LONDON AND NEW YORK

Designed cover image: © Getty Images

First published 2023
by Routledge
4 Park Square, Milton Park, Abingdon, Oxon OX14 4RN

and by Routledge
605 Third Avenue, New York, NY 10158

Routledge is an imprint of the Taylor & Francis Group, an informa business

© 2023 Megan E. Birney

The right of Megan E. Birney to be identified as author of this work has been asserted in accordance with sections 77 and 78 of the Copyright, Designs and Patents Act 1988.

British Library Cataloguing-in-Publication Data
A catalogue record for this book is available from the British Library

ISBN: 9780367223649 (hbk)
ISBN: 9780367223656 (pbk)
ISBN: 9780429274534 (ebk)

DOI: 10.4324/9780429274534

Typeset in Bembo
by codeMantra

To Jason, Piran, Lowen, and Eliza. You have shaped my self and identity more than you could ever know

CONTENTS

1

DEFINING THE SELF

BOX 1.1 WHO AM I?

Ask yourself the question, "Who am I?" then write down the first five things that come to your mind. Try not to spend more than a couple of minutes deciding what to write.

Who am I? At some point or another, most everyone has asked themselves this question. If you took part in the activity in Box 1.1, there is huge variety in the answers you could have given. You might have listed your family role or your job title. You might have described your personality, your hobbies, or stated demographics such as your nationality, religion, or gender identity. You might have written your name.

The ability to reflect on who we are is something that makes human beings unique from other mammals. In the same way that you don't have to understand how the respiratory system works to breathe, selfhood is automatic for most animals. For humans, however, the question, 'who am I?' is one that anthropologists believe we've been grappling with since our days as hunters and gatherers (Edwardes, 2019). Yet there remains no universal definition of the self, nor is there an agreed consensus about what exactly selfhood is. Still, the concept of self and the theorising around it has shaped disciplines ranging from theology to biology to political science, to name a few.

DOI: 10.4324/9780429274534-1

As we will see from this chapter, the literature on the self is vast. It spans thousands of years and covers what feels like just as many perspectives! In this book, we take a specific view of the self: drawing on the field of social psychology, we examine selfhood using the social identity approach (Tajfel & Turner, 1979; Turner et al., 1987). But before we delve into this view, we will spend this chapter touching on just some of the different perspectives of the self from Western philosophy and psychology. We will then consider modern beliefs about the self (i.e., true self beliefs) and how these influence our thinking and our behaviour. Importantly, the conceptual frameworks provided in this chapter will help to set the stage for the rest of this book where we will be thinking about the self as a function of identity.

PHILOSOPHICAL NOTIONS OF THE SELF

One area that has had a clear impact on our understanding of self-hood is Western philosophy. After all, quotes referring to the self, such as 'Know thyself' (Socrates 470–399 BC) and 'I think, therefore I am' (Descartes 1596–1650), have been known in popular culture for centuries. Before we delve into some of these ideas, it is important to note that in this literature, the terminology used to describe selfhood varies: the word 'self' can refer to our biological existence, the word 'mind' might describe the part of us that perceives stimulus and initiates action, and the word 'soul' often includes our religion or moral compass. When considering the context in which these words were used, it is likely that they all referred to what we'd describe today as selfhood (see Perry, 2013). In philosophical terms, the soul, the mind, and the self all describe our ability to think, that is, to reason, to analyse, and to imagine. Unlike the body, which is constantly changing, the 'self' is believed to stay relatively stable. From this perspective, it is the self that makes up our being.

A (very!) short overview of key ideas in Western philosophical thinking about the self demonstrates how complex the ideas about selfhood are. One concept of self is that of *dualism*, the idea that humans consist of both the body and the soul, and that the two exist independently from each other. It is believed that Socrates (470– 399 BC) saw the soul as the moral and intellectual essence of human beings. He emphasised the importance of self-examination and the acquisition of knowledge to live a meaningful life (i.e., the 'good life' as he called it). This idea is articulated in his famous quote "The unexamined life is not worth living." In what was revolutionary for the time, Socrates believed the state of one's soul was more important than material riches, status, or reputation.

Socrates's student, Plato (428/427–348/347 BC), largely agreed with him but took the concept of the soul as a separate entity from the body further. He argued that humans have three souls: the rational soul which allows you to reason, the spiritual soul which gives you emotion, and the appetitive soul which regulates your body's basic needs. For him, the rational soul is superior because it can control the other two. To illustrate this, imagine you are out on a walk, and you start to feel cold. You pass someone who has a coat for sale, but you don't have any money with you. The fact that you would continue to feel cold rather than stealing the coat is an example of your rational soul superseding the spiritual and appetitive souls. For Plato, the rational soul is one's true self and, importantly, can live forever; after the body dies, it finds another body to inhabit. These ideas mirror those of *reincarnation*, the belief that a being's spirit inhabits another body upon death.

Other famous dualists include Augustine (AD 354–430) who's thinking on the self would have been heavily influenced by the advent of modern Christianity. Sainted by the Catholic church in 1303, St. Augustine believed that while the soul is immortal, it does not inhabit different bodies as suggested by Plato. Rather, the soul unites with the body to complete us as human beings. Because he believed that humans were created in God's image, he believed that the only way to really know and understand one's self is to know and understand God. Nearly 2,000 years later, another famous philosopher, Rene Descartes (1596–1650), would take a different approach in his reasoning for the existence of a separate mind and body. Famous in part for his rational approach to questions and as the creator of deductive reasoning, Descartes acknowledged that, because the mind cannot be observed, it is impossible to study it objectively. For Descartes then, proof of the mind's existence lies in our ability to doubt. He claimed that even if we are tricked into believing that we are not real, the fact that we have these thought processes at all proves that our self is, in fact, a real entity.

Not everyone subscribed to the concept of dualism. Plato's own student, Aristotle (384–322 BC), disagreed about the body's connection to the soul. For him, the soul is a form of the body; it is what gives the body life and, therefore, it dies when the body dies. He argued that all living things have a soul: plants have a vegetative soul that allows them to grow and reproduce, animals have a sensitive soul which gives them feeling and sensation, and humans have a rational soul which is unique in giving us the ability to think. Much later, David Hume (1711–1776) would take a different stance entirely on the question of how the self is relevant to the body. For him, the self is not real. Rather, it is an illusion and only exists through the senses. He argued that although we have a concept of the self, this does not mean that the self is real. In what some might consider a compromise between Aristotle and Hume are the ideas put forward by Immanuel Kant (1724–1804). Kant claimed that we have an 'inner self' (i.e., our rational thought) and an 'outer self' (i.e., our senses) that make up who we are. For him, these two selves unite to make us aware of our moral obligations.

Recent theorising about selfhood has considered the emphasis in modern day on how the individual relates to their own thinking and observations of the world. One particularly influential modern philosopher is Charles Taylor. According to Taylor (1989), who we are is determined by our morality. Importantly, selfhood is established not just from acting moral but by *being* moral. In this way, we cannot separate who we are from what we consider to be good or right. Of course, our morality depends on our perspective or 'framework' (i.e., what we consider to be good and how we relate to that good). As an example, one of the five 'British values' taught in British schools involves 'tolerance of those with different backgrounds or faiths.' For people in Britain then, this framework might guide moral thinking and, by extension, selfhood. From Taylor's perspective, this helps to explain why religion tends to play such an important role in determining how we conceptualise the self, as it is often religion that guides our moral framework. Even if we don't subscribe to a particular religion as an individual, we are still influenced by the religious make-up within our culture.

Interestingly, at least from a social psychological perspective, is the emphasis Taylor places on the role of others. For him, morality (and hence the self) is intertwined with our obligation to others in our social world. For instance, someone who has a talent for teaching has a moral obligation to use that talent for the betterment of others. He also acknowledges that others validate us and, as such, play an essential role in helping us realise who we are. For instance, losing your framework (because of rejecting church teachings, for example) or failing to have one's self acknowledged by others can lead to intense feelings of confusion. This idea – that who we are is dependent on other people – is an overarching theme in this book.

PSYCHOLOGICAL NOTIONS OF THE SELF

One key contribution of psychology to our understanding of the self is its use of empirical testing. Through this, psychologists have evidenced the influence that external factors, such as unconscious bias and social conditioning, have on who we are (Sparby et al., 2019). Still, there remains no agreed definition of the self within the field. Depending on your view, selfhood can be subjective based on what we are individually aware of (e.g., the experiential perspective), our genetics (e.g., the biological perspective), or the way we have been rewarded and punished throughout our lives (e.g., the behaviourist perspective). It might also emerge from unconscious thought (e.g., the psychodynamic perspective) or be constructed from messages received from society (e.g., the social constructionist perspective; Stevens, 1996). Yet, even within these perspectives, the literature on the self is vast. Take social psychology as an example: in *The Handbook of Social Psychology* (Fiske et al., 2010), the index contains over 60 entries for the word 'self' (Strohminger et al., 2017).

Psychology's theorising about selfhood starts with one of the field's first ever books, *Principles of Psychology* by William James (1890). In his seminal chapter about the self, James separates the *I* (as a subject) and the *Me* (as an object). He proposes that the *I* acts as an administrator for the *Me* in that it controls, critiques, develops, and represents it (McAdams & Cox, 2010). James proposed that the *I* reflects on itself to gain an understanding of who and what it is. For instance, if I find myself feeling nervous in social situations, my *I* might conclude that my *Me* is shy. Of course, much of what it uses to interpret the *Me* comes from the social world. James proposed that, in addition to a *material Me* (e.g., our home and possessions) and a *spiritual Me* (i.e., how we perceive our abilities, values, and motives), we all have a *social Me* that is concerned with how we are seen by others. This includes not only our actual reputation but our perception of what others think about us. As most of us can probably relate, this latter concern – how we *think* we are seen by those around us – can be just as (if not more) important as people's actual opinions. In this book, we take an approach that considers the *social Me* as paramount for determining selfhood.

Perhaps psychology's most well-known theory of the self is Sigmund Freud's (1923) psychoanalytic theory. Freud believed that we face constant conflict between three different selves that each have different needs. The *Id* is our drive for immediate satisfaction without regard for consequences; it is primal and animalistic in nature. The *Super Ego* sets out what is usually an unattainable standard of law and morality. The *Ego* is our rationale thought and negotiates between the two. To illustrate how this works, imagine that you are hungry. The *Id* might tempt you to binge on chocolate while the *Super Ego* might berate you for even considering eating an unhealthy food. The *Ego* is faced with reconciling these two competing selves, a challenge made even more difficult by the varying states of consciousness each self exists in. For Freud, the *Id* is unconscious, while the *Ego* and the *Super Ego* operate at both the conscious and the unconscious level. Although Freud pioneered the idea that we are often unaware of key elements ourself, he still acknowledged the importance of others. As an example, he described the *Ego* as "that part of the id which has been modified by the direct influence of the social world" (Freud, 1923).

The final theory we will detail in this section is Erik Erikson's eight stages of psychosocial development. Erikson (1963) proposed that who we are is a constant balance between our psychological needs as individuals and the demands of our social world. Between infancy and older age, people are faced with various challenges (or *crisis* as he called them) that must be resolved to maintain a healthy *Ego*. This is particularly difficult during adolescence when young people are transitioning from childhood to adulthood. Because young people are facing questions about everything from their future occupation to their sexuality to their politics, Erikson theorised that it is during this 'crisis' that the question 'who am I?' surfaces for the first time. To facilitate an answer, teenagers may try out different personas and experiment with playing new roles within their social worlds – sometimes to their parents' dismay! While the "who am I?" question may never truly get resolved (McAdams & Cox, 2010), completion of this stage is marked by a virtue that Erikson called *fidelity*, which he described as "the ability to sustain loyalties pledged in spite of inevitable contradiction of value systems" (Erikson, 1963). In other words, the best outcome of this stage is that young people emerge secure enough with who they are to maintain genuine relationships with others and to feel a part of their communities.

Humanistic notions of selfhood contrast these earlier ideas with more optimism about the self. Rather than seeing the self as in constant conflict or as facing constant crisis, humanists proposed that a true self lives within all of us. While uncovering it requires hard work and perseverance, success results in joy and feeling satisfied within our lives. Today, belief in the existence of a true self (or *true self beliefs*) is embedded in our thinking, not just in the West but around the world (Strohminger et al., 2017). In the next section, we consider how believing in a true self guides our beliefs and our behaviours, both of which influence who we are. Indeed, we will be revisiting this cyclical relationship between what we believe about our self and how we think and behave throughout this book.

TRUE SELF BELIEFS

One challenge when discussing the self is that it's a word that describes multiple concepts. Writings in both philosophy and psychology use it to refer to both the mass of cells that make up our bodies (i.e., what happens "within the skin"; Gilbert & Malone, 1995) and another self that consists of our essence. This latter concept is known as the 'true self,' but is sometimes called the 'real self,' the 'essential self,' and the 'ideal self,' among others. Defining the true self is difficult (see Baumeister, 2019), but we can think of it as the part of us that feels authentic. Belief in the existence of a true self echoes some of the ideas outlined in the previous section: when realised, the true self leads us to a fulfilling life (Strohminger et al., 2017). If you think about it, you likely believe in a true self without necessarily being aware of it. For instance, have you ever given the advice to "be yourself?" Or decided to forgive another person because you believe that whatever they did was not reflective of who they *really* are? As we will see in this section, the idea that people have a true self permeate our everyday thinking and, as such, guide how we navigate the social world.

Popular culture is rife with examples of a 'true self.' One that is often used in texts about the self is *Alice in Wonderland*. This classic story makes numerous references to different themes related to selfhood. Consider when the Caterpillar asks Alice, "Who are you?" and Alice answers, "I – I hardly know, Sir, just at present – at least I know who I was when I got up this morning, but I think I must have changed several times since then" (Carroll, 1865). Exemplifying Charles Taylor's emphasis on the importance of one's moral framework in shaping their self, this scene illustrates how a change in our social world can alter our understanding of who we are. References to the existence of a 'true self' can be found in movies from *The Matrix* (where Neo embarks on a journey that finds him discovering a genuine existence), *A Christmas Carol* (where Ebenezer Scrooge transforms from his miserly ways to a true self that is generous and empathetic) to *Grease* (where Sandy leaves her true innocent and sweet self behind to impress her peers with a new bad girl image). The idea that each of us has a 'true self' is a prevalent theme within many areas in society, from wellness advice to television commercials (Rivera et al., 2019).

One theme underlying these portrayals is that people's true self is both good and moral. Generally, positive behaviours are perceived as reflecting who a person truly is; when a person's behaviour goes from negative to positive, it is seen less as a change and more as an uncovering of their true self (Bench et al., 2015). Conversely, negative behaviours are generally attributed to a person's surface or 'false self' (Newman et al., 2014). The importance of virtue as a part of the true self becomes clear when you consider that, more than other traits, morality is believed to be at the core of who we are (Prinz & Nichols, 2016). It is also the most important factor in shaping our impressions of others (Goodwin, 2015). Of course, whether a behaviour is considered moral depends on perspective. A person who believes that abortion is wrong will be more likely to attribute the decision not to have one as reflecting a woman's true self compared to someone without such views. Along these same lines, research has found that people who identify as liberal are more likely to view sexual attraction to a person of their same sex as reflecting one's true self compared to people with other ideologies (Newman et al., 2014).

While some evidence suggests that we see our own true selves as superior to others' (Zhang & Alicke, 2021), we tend to believe that all true selves are good and moral. These convictions appear in both Western and Eastern cultures; while there may be variations between which behaviours are considered moral and good, the belief in a righteous true self seems universal (Strohminger et al., 2017). Given how prevalent these beliefs are, the implications they have for our thoughts, feelings, and behaviours are immense. For instance, because true selves are understood as fundamental within human beings (Christy et al., 2019), and these are assumed to be both good and moral, we may be inclined to give others the benefit of the doubt. In other words, if we believe that a person's negative or immoral behaviours do not represent who they really are, we might feel it is right to forgive them, even if they have acted abhorrently. The excuses made available by the supposed existence of a true self can also be applied to our own behaviours: our belief that our true self is more virtuous than our actual self (Newman et al., 2015) gives us a reason to minimise our own poor behaviour because we can rationalise that a better person lives within us.

From a more positive perspective, it is also possible that a belief in a good and moral true self means that we strive for our actions to uphold that standard (Rivera et al., 2019). Researchers have pointed to several benefits that can be gained when people feel in touch with their true selves, including greater resilience (Wickham et al., 2016), stronger relationships (Baker et al., 2017), and higher motivation (Kim et al., 2017). There is also evidence that when we believe we have been guided by our true selves, we feel more confident in our decisions (Kim et al., 2021). While many of us will recognise the positive emotions that come with feelings of authenticity, the implications of true self beliefs can also have more subtle consequences for our actions. For instance, Strohminger and colleagues (2017) argue that these beliefs might explain people's reluctance to take medication designed to regulate traits that are seen as integral to the true self (e.g., mood) but show less hesitancy taking medication to improve traits considered more peripheral, such as concentration or memory (Riis et al., 2008).

The literature on true self beliefs exemplifies a key theme within the social identity approach to understanding the self: how we perceive our self and others plays an integral role in shaping how we think, feel, and behave. In the next section, we break down some key aspects of the self and consider how these relate to the social world.

SELF AND IDENTITY

Most of us can probably observe that our self is subject to constant change. Whatever your perspective is on selfhood, who you are as a child is not the same as who you are as an adult. Even in adulthood, most of us would agree that when we experience a major life event, such as becoming a parent or experiencing trauma, we feel changed somehow, compared to who we were before the event. At any given time, how we think about our self, or what we think about who we are, relies on our *self-concept*. This might include aspects of our personality (e.g., I'm funny), our feelings (e.g., I'm sad), and our beliefs (I'm a liberal; Oyserman et al., 2012). When thinking of your answer to the question "Who am I?", you might have engaged in further reflection, for instance, through questions such as 'How do I know who I am?' and 'How do I feel about myself?' The concepts that these questions tap into (e.g., outside influences and our self-esteem) intertwine to give us a sense of what makes us unique as an individual. Your answers to these have also probably changed over the course of your life: my responses to these questions 20 years ago are not the same as how I would answer them how. This is because our experiences have a profound impact on who we are: our view of the world, our priorities, and, by extension, our self.

It is these experiences that result in what psychologists call as our self-schemas. A *schema* is an important concept in psychology. It is defined as a cognitive structure that represents our understanding of a concept or social stimulus (Fiske & Taylor, 1991). Schemas serve as cognitive shortcuts that help us make sense of all the stimuli we are faced with as we navigate our social world. When confronted with social stimuli, we only have limited information and limited time to process that information, so we rely on schemas to guide our thinking. Generally, we develop our schemas from previous experiences and by accumulating cultural knowledge. For instance, you may have never attended a lecture at university before, and yet, on the first day, you were aware of how you should behave in one. Likewise, if you are invited to a birthday party, you know a present may be expected without this being explicitly stated. Schemas come in different forms: *person schemas* contain your knowledge about specific people (e.g., Dads like to tell bad jokes), *role schemas* represent your knowledge about what is appropriate based on people's positions (e.g., your lecturer can teach you, but not shout at you), and *event schemas* include your knowledge about how to behave while in your immediate social environment (e.g., you can scream at a football match, but not while travelling on the train).

As you can probably guess, *self-schemas* contain the specific knowledge we have about our self. Like other schemas, these are influenced by the social world in which we live. To illustrate the power of this relationship, ask yourself to describe a university student. Some characteristics that come to mind might include the following: students revise and attend lectures. They are young. They sleep in late. They go on nights out and drink alcohol. They eat baked beans and pot noodles. You may have listed these attributes without much thought because they are in line with many people's person schemas regarding students. But now, consider whether your list describes you as a student *personally*. From my perspective as an academic, this description does not apply to most students. Many of the students I've worked with over the past 10 years are not regularly staying out late drinking, nor are they sleeping until noon. Rather, they have sacrificed a lot to come to university and take their opportunity for education seriously. They are balancing their course commitments with paid work and family life. Increasing numbers are middle-aged and older and are returning to education after gaining invaluable life experiences. Still, the caricature of young, partying, students is largely accepted, even among the members of this group that embody the opposite!

Knowledge gained from the social world feed our self-schemas, which, in turn, make up our self-concept. As in the example above, an older student might not be as proud of this part of their self because of their person schema that university students have just finished school. Hence, they might feel they are somehow behind their younger colleagues. In many ways, our self-schemas are tied to our *self-esteem* or, how we evaluate ourselves as positive or negative (Rosenberg, 1979). Researchers generally categorise self-esteem along two dimensions: *efficacy-based self-esteem* is the extent that we see our self as capable, while *worth-based self-esteem* is concerned with feeling valued and accepted (Gecas & Schwalbe, 1983). Just as our self-schemas inform our self-esteem, our self-esteem informs our self-schemas. For instance, if you have a self-schema that you are bad at sport, but you desire to be athletic, this discrepancy can result in lower self-esteem (Higgins et al., 1986). The consequences we experience when our self-concept is not in line with what we hope to be is discussed in Chapter 2.

Of course, we do not think about our self all the time. Rather, we experience different levels of *self-awareness* depending on factors such as our personality and the situation we are in. Broadly, self-awareness describes the attention we devote to our self (Carver, 2003) and can be divided into two main types: *private self-awareness* describes our interpersonal perceptions, while *public self-awareness* is our beliefs about the way others see us. Being self-aware can have a number of benefits. For instance, imagine you have just had a fight with a friend. Engaging in private self-awareness might help you make sense of the conflict and gain insight into your emotions and behaviours. Engaging in public self-awareness might help you see the conflict from the perspective of your friend. Both play a role in helping you move on from the situation. Research has also found that engaging in private self-awareness can lead to happiness, feelings of control, and life satisfaction, while being publicly self-aware promotes greater empathy and stronger relationships with others (Eurich, 2018). However, self-awareness can also contribute to depression and anxiety: pre-occupation with one's internal state or obsessive worry about others' opinions can be detrimental to mental health (Silvia & O'Brien, 2004). Either way, self-awareness helps shape our self-concept.

This leads us to the other term in the title of this book: *Identity*. While the terms 'self' and 'identity' are often used interchangeably, they are distinct concepts. Identity refers to various aspects of one's self-concept. For instance, if your answer to the question 'Who am I?' included 'sister,' you would be drawing on your role identity. If you described yourself as a 'Christian,' that would be your religious identity. In sum, our identities are the parts of us that are tied to the social structure in which we exist and consist of our traits, roles, social relations, and group memberships (Oyserman et al., 2012). However, the concept of identity goes further than this because it also encompasses the meaning of the roles that we play. For instance, what does it *mean* to be a sister? Or a Christian? Our answers to these will come from our social world and, in turn, will inform our thoughts and behaviours.

In this book, we define identity in line with that of the American Psychological Association: "an individual's sense of self defined by (a) a set of physical, psychological, and interpersonal characteristics that is not wholly shared with any other person and (b) a range of affiliations (e.g., ethnicity) and social roles" (APA, 2022). Our identity impacts on how we think, feel, and behave, and how we think, feel, and behave is impacted by our social world. Unlike schemas, which act as structures within our cognition, how we identify with something falls along a continuum. For instance, if you play the guitar, you might identify as a musician. For some, this identity may not be particularly important, but as something they do, or used to do, as a hobby. For others, being a musician feels at the core of who they are; they can't fathom being or doing anything else. We can also identify with others and the causes those others represent. Our musician may be particularly likely to identify with a band who has a guitarist they admire because of the identity they share. In this way, identity can be thought of as our expression of the relationship we have with what is happening around us. This relationship consists of what we know about our self, the claims we make about our self, and the recognition we get from others (Chryssochoou, 2003). Hence, our identities, and by extension our self, are inherently social.

CONCLUSION

Human thinking about the self is vast. Yet despite the different ways the self has been conceptualised, there are at least three key features of selfhood that all scholars are likely to agree on. One is that selfhood is a complex concept, encompassing many aspects of our state of existence. Another is that having an awareness of self, and the ability to distinguish one's self from the self of others, is necessary for human functioning (Edwardes, 2019). A third, and perhaps most relevant to this book, is that our self is influenced by other people. While this observation may be something you've noticed when reflecting on your own self, empirical evidence alone leaves little doubt that one's social world plays a key role in shaping who they are (Sparby et al., 2019).

In this book, we view the self through identity processes. Two key themes underpin this perspective: (1) our thoughts, behaviours, and beliefs are impacted by who and what we identify with; and (2) who and what we identify are affected by our thoughts, behaviours, and beliefs. Chapter 2 delves deeper into the idea that who we are depends on others and will set out the key ways in which humans interact as group members. In Chapter 3, we look at two key theoretical approaches to understanding self and identity: the social identity approach and intersectionality. Chapter 4 focuses on the influences others have on how we act in specific situations, while Chapter 5 examines how the relationship between different groups affects our individual self-concept. Finally, Chapter 6 looks at the role that language and communication play in shaping who we are. We conclude with Chapter 7 where we consider how the themes presented in this book are relevant to organizational structures. These chapters work together to offer a comprehensive picture of the social psychology of self and identity.

CHAPTER SUMMARY

- Ideas about selfhood are vast, spanning thousands of years. This book examines the self from a social identity perspective which considers the self as a function of how and what a person identifies with.
- Although psychological notions of selfhood vary, they all acknowledge the importance of other people in shaping who we are.
- There is a tendency to believe that we all have a true, authentic self that is moral and good. This belief shapes our thoughts, feelings, and behaviours towards both others and ourselves.
- How we answer the question 'Who am I?' is made up of many factors: how we think about our various social roles, how we feel about ourselves, and how we view those around us.
- Identity describes the parts of us that are tied to the social world. How we think about these identities and how we identify with others around us impact on our self-concept.

WANT TO KNOW MORE?

Recommended Reading:

- Chryssochoou, X. (2003). Studying identity in social psychology: Some thoughts on the definition of identity and its relation to action. *Journal of language and Politics, 2*(2), 225–241. https://doi.org/10.1075/jlp.2.2.03chr
- Leary, M. R., & Tangney, J. P. (Eds.). (2012). *Handbook of self and identity*. Guilford Press
- McAdams, D. P., & Cox, K. S. (2010). Self and identity across the life span. In M. E. Lamb & A. M. Freund (Eds.), *The handbook of life-span development: Vol. 2. Social and emotional development* (pp. 158–207). Wiley

REFERENCES

APA. (2022). *APA dictionary of psychology*. https://dictionary.apa.org/identity

Baker, Z. G., Tou, R. Y., Bryan, J. L., & Knee, C. R. (2017). Authenticity and well-being: Exploring positivity and negativity in interactions as a mediator. *Personality and Individual Differences, 113*, 235–239. http://doi.org/10.1016/j.paid.2017.03.018

Baumeister, R. F. (2019). Stalking the true self through the jungles of authenticity: Problems, contradictions, inconsistencies, disturbing findings—And a possible way forward. *Review of General Psychology, 23*(1), 143–154. https://doi.org/10.1177/1089268019829472

Bench, S. W., Schlegel, R. J., Davis, W. E., & Vess, M. (2015). Thinking about change in the self and others: The role of self-discovery metaphors and the true self. *Social Cognition, 33*(3), 169. https://doi.org/10.1521/soco.2015.33.3.2

Carroll, L. 1865 [1982]. Alice's adventures in wonderland. In *The Complete Illustrated Works of Lewis Carroll*. Chancellor Press

Carver, C. S. (2003). Self-awareness. In M. R. Leary & J. P. Tangney (Eds.), *Handbook of self and identity* (pp. 179–196). Guilford

Christy, A. G., Schlegel, R. J., & Cimpian, A. (2019). Why do people believe in a "true self"? The role of essentialist reasoning about personal identity and the self. *Journal of Personality and Social Psychology, 117*(2), 386. https://doi.org/10.1037/pspp0000254

Chryssochoou, X. (2003). Studying identity in social psychology: Some thoughts on the definition of identity and its relation to action. *Journal of Language and Politics, 2*(2), 225–241. https://doi.org/10.1075/jlp.2.2.03chr

Edwardes, M. P. J. (2019). *The origins of self: An anthropological perspective*. UCL Press.

Erikson, E. H. (1963). *Childhood and society* (2nd Ed.). Norton

Eurich, T. (2018). What self-awareness really is (and how to cultivate it). *Harvard Business Review, 2,* 1–9

Fiske, S. T., Gilbert, D. T., & Lindzey, G. (2010). *Handbook of social psychology* (5th Ed., Vol. 2). John Wiley & Sons

Fiske, S. T., & Taylor, S. E. (1991). *Social cognition.* Mcgraw-Hill Book Company

Freud, S. (1923/1961). The ego and the id. In J. Strachey (Ed.), *The standard edition of the complete psychological works of Sigmund Freud* (Vol. 19). Hogarth

Gecas, V., & Schwalbe, M. L. (1983). Beyond the looking-glass self: Social structure and efficacy-based self-esteem. *Social Psychology Quarterly, 46,* 77–88. https://doi.org/10.2307/3033844

Gilbert, D. T., & Malone, P. S. (1995). The correspondence bias. *Psychological Bulletin, 117*(1), 21–38. https://doi.org/10.1037/0033-2909.117.1.21

Goodwin, G. P. (2015). Moral character in person perception. *Current Directions in Psychological Science, 24*(1), 38–44. https://doi.org/10.1177/0963721414550709

Higgins, E. T., Bond, R. N., Klein, R., & Strauman, T. (1986). Self-discrepancies and emotional vulnerability: How magnitude, accessibility, and type of discrepancy influence affect. *Journal of Personality and Social Psychology, 51*(1), 5–15. https://doi.org/10.1037/0022-3514.51.1.5

Kim, J., Christy, A. G., Rivera, G. N., Hicks, J. A., & Schlegel, R. J. (2021). Is the illusion of authenticity beneficial? Merely perceiving decisions as guided by the true self enhances decision satisfaction. *Social Psychological and Personality Science, 12*(1), 80–90. https://doi.org/10.1177/1948550620903202

Kim, J., Christy, A. G., Schlegel, R. J., Donnellan, M. B., & Hicks, J. A. (2017). Existential ennui: Examining the reciprocal relationship between self-alienation and academic amotivation. *Social Psychological and Personality Science, 9*(7), 853–862. http://dx.doi.org/10.1177/1948550617727587

McAdams, D. P., & Cox, K. S. (2010). Self and identity across the life span. In M. E. Lamb & A. M. Freund (Eds.), *The handbook of life-span development: Vol. 2. Social and emotional development* (pp. 158–207). Wiley

Newman, G. E., Bloom, P., & Knobe, J. (2014). Value judgments and the true self. *Personality and Social Psychology Bulletin, 40*(2), 203–216. https://doi.org/10.1177/0146167213508791

Newman, G. E., De Freitas, J., & Knobe, J. (2015). Beliefs about the true self explain asymmetries based on moral judgment. *Cognitive Science, 39*(1), 96–125. https://doi.org/10.1111/cogs.12134

Oyserman, D., Elmore, K., & Smith, G. (2012). Self, self-concept, and identity. In M. R. Leary, & J. P. Tangney (Eds.), *Handbook of self and identity* (pp. 69–104). Routledge

Perry, J. (2013, February 21). The self. *Philosophy Talk*. https://www.philosophytalk.org/blog/self

Prinz, J., & Nichols, S. (2016). Diachronic identity and the moral self. In J. Kiverstein (Ed.), *The Routledge handbook of philosophy of the social mind* (pp. 449–464). Routledge

Riis, J., Simmons, J. P., & Goodwin, G. P. (2008). Preferences for enhancement pharmaceuticals: The reluctance to enhance fundamental traits. *Journal of Consumer Research, 35*(3), 495–508. https://doi.org/10.1086/588746

Rivera, G. N., Christy, A. G., Kim, J., Vess, M., Hicks, J. A., & Schlegel, R. J. (2019). Understanding the relationship between perceived authenticity and well-being. *Review of General Psychology, 23*(1), 113–126. https://doi.org/10.1037/gpr0000161

Rosenberg, M. (1979). *Conceiving the self*. Basic Books

Silvia, P. J., & O'Brien, M. E. (2004). Self-awareness and constructive functioning: Revisiting "the human dilemma". *Journal of Social and Clinical Psychology, 23*(4), 475–489. https://doi.org/10.1521/jscp.23.4.475.40307

Sparby, T., Edelhäuser, F., & Weger, U. W. (2019). The true self. Critique, nature, and method. *Frontiers in Psychology, 10*, 2250. https://doi.org/10.3389/fpsyg.2019.02250

Stevens, R. (1996). *Understanding the self*. Sage

Strohminger, N., Knobe, J., & Newman, G. (2017). The true self: A psychological concept distinct from the self. *Perspectives on Psychological Science, 12*(4), 551–560. https://doi.org/10.1177/1745691616689495

Tajfel, H., & Turner, J. C. (1979). An integrative theory of intergroup conflict. In W. G. Austin & S. Worchel (Eds.), *The social psychology of intergroup relations* (pp. 33–48). Brooks/Cole

Turner, J. C., Hogg, M. A., Oakes, P. J., Reicher, S. D., & Wetherell, M. S. (1987). *Rediscovering the social group: A self-categorization theory*. Blackwell

Wickham, R. E., Williamson, R. E., Beard, C. L., Kobayashi, C. L., & Hirst, T. W. (2016). Authenticity attenuates the negative effects of interpersonal conflict on daily well-being. *Journal of Research in Personality, 60*, 56–62. http://dx.doi.org/10.1016/j.jrp.2015.11.006

Zhang, Y., & Alicke, M. (2021). My true self is better than yours: Comparative bias in true self judgments. *Personality and Social Psychology Bulletin, 47*(2), 216–231. https://doi.org/10.1177/0146167220919213

THE SELF AS A SOCIAL RELATIONSHIP

Who we are depends on others. Not only do others guide how we see our self, but they shape how we appear to others through their influence of our thoughts, beliefs, and behaviours. How we think and act, in turn, further shape how we view our self. Think about when you got dressed this morning. Whether you thought about it or not, your choice of clothing was influenced by others in your social world. If you were dressing for work, you probably chose attire deemed appropriate for your workplace. If you were dressing to go out with friends, you might have dressed more in line with the latest fashions. Even while shopping for the clothes that make up your wardrobe, what you choose to buy is largely determined by how you want to express yourself to those who will see you. How we present our self is not only a reflection of our personal self-concept but is determined by how we want others to see us and how we think others see us. In this way, the relationship between our perception of self and the influence of others is cyclical.

At the most basic level, others are necessary for maintaining our overall health and well-being. For humans, relationships form easily; in many instances, just having regular exposure to another person is all we need to form a social bond with them (Kawakami & Yoshida, 2015). Research shows that there is much to benefit from the relationships we form; people who are active across broader social networks have been found to adjust better to change (Steffens et al., 2016), are more resilient (Jones & Jetten, 2011), and may even live longer (Holt-Lunstad et al., 2017). In one compelling study, Cohen and colleagues (1997) asked healthy adults about their

DOI: 10.4324/9780429274534-2

social networks before exposing them to the cold virus under quarantined conditions. Across several different illness criteria, those with stronger social connections were less affected by the virus. It seems then that others help keep us happy and healthy, both of which are important for the way we maintain our sense of self.

However, our reliance on others may go even deeper than supporting our health. According to Baumeister and Leary (1995), the need to belong to groups of others is fundamental. Without it, humans are unable to maintain normal psychological functioning. Supporting this premise, research has shown that group membership is necessary for satisfying our basic need to belong, to maintain self-esteem, to exercise control over our outcomes, and to believe that our existence has meaning (Greenaway et al., 2016). Like other social creatures, it is possible that humans evolved this need as a means of survival. Indeed, organisms who are more socially integrated are more likely to survive to adulthood, to reproduce, and to successfully produce offspring (Nowak & Highfield, 2011). From an evolutionary standpoint therefore, it is clearly advantageous to have and to maintain social connections.

Because our social connections are necessary for psychological functioning, the loss of these connections can be deeply distressing. As many of us can probably relate, few things are more painful than the loss of a relationship: whether it's a break-up with a romantic partner, a fall-out with a friend, or the dissolution of a friendship group. This pain seems so universal that you'd be hard-pressed to turn on the radio and not find a song about it! Research suggests that the pain we feel from rejection is not just emotional. In a neuroimaging study, Eisenberger and colleagues (2003) found that the brain activity in participants experiencing social exclusion was like that of those experiencing physical pain. This may help to explain why the idea of ending up alone in life has consequences (e.g., lower cognitive functioning) that go beyond those of other negative life experiences (e.g., physical injury; Baumeister et al., 2002).

Because the consequences of rejection are so acute, we often to go to great lengths to resist the loss of relationships, even when these are meaningless or even disliked (Gonsalkorale & Williams, 2007). For instance, imagine that all the students in your psychology class formed a study group but did not ask you to join. Even if you didn't care much for the people in your class, not being included would probably still sting. In fact, social exclusion, or *ostracism*, is one of the most distressing experiences we can have. It also serves as a common form of punishment. Imagine that you have a friend who you feel has betrayed you. In response to that betrayal, you might stop speaking to them. Consider when a child acts in an unacceptable way. A common response is to have that child spend a fixed amount of time by themselves (i.e., in 'time-out'). Both responses are a form of ostracism because you are either permanently or temporarily cutting the person off from a social connection. Because we have evolved as a species to depend on others for survival (think of how ancient humans had to band together just to survive!), we are inclined both to use ostracism as a punishment and to be hypersensitive to it (hence the extreme pain we feel when it happens to us.). In this way, ostracism serves to regulate the behaviour of ourselves and others.

The experience of ostracism and the strategies we employ to avoid ostracism help shape who we are. Research suggests that people's responses to ostracism seem paradoxical; we either attempt to ingratiate ourselves by making a concerted effort to blend in or we become more antisocial and aggressive (Wesselmann et al., 2015). The strategy we choose may depend on the psychological function we need to fulfil (the former response helps us meet our need for belonging and self-esteem, while the latter response helps us meet our need for control and to see meaning in our lives; Williams, 2009). Either way, our need to be included by others drives who we are by shaping our thoughts and our behaviours. In other words, the dependency we have on others for our basic psychological functioning and survival means that we cannot consider who we are without also considering those who share our social world.

Although our response to ostracism plays a fundamental role in determining who we are, it is perhaps one of the more extreme examples of the role that others play in shaping our self-concept. The more mundane interactions we have within our everyday lives also serve this function. One example of this is the tendency for people to shift towards more extreme views after engaging in conversation with like-minded others (Moscovici & Zavalloni, 1969). Known as *group polarisation*, the phenomenon has been demonstrated across several domains, from jury decisions to terrorism to political ideologies (Broncano-Berrocal & Carter, 2020). Researchers have suggested several explanations for this shift in our thinking. One of these is *social comparison theory* which posits that we define who we are by comparing ourselves to others (Festinger, 1954). This includes gauging our own beliefs from those around us. Not only do we prefer to compare ourselves to others with similar opinions (Suls & Wheeler, 2000), but we often assume that our opinions are more extreme than the group average (Broncano-Berrocal & Carter, 2020). We then tend to present them as such during conversations with like-minded others, resulting in everyone being exposed to more extreme positions of the topic. Because we ground our thinking based on the thinking of others, this has the influence of shifting our views towards that extreme – often without us realising it!

So far, we have introduced some of the most fundamental ways that others shape who we are. Over the rest of this chapter, we will delve deeper into theories that help explain the influence others have on our self. We begin by considering the role of individuals on our self-concept before exploring the influence of our group membership and our culture. We end the chapter by considering these ideas within the framework of our social identities.

OTHERS AS A POINT OF SELF-COMPARISON

Others shape our sense of self by validating our experiences. Having our experiences validated, in turn, guides our feelings and our behaviours. Imagine you are in your first year at university and are taking a statistics class. If you are like many new students, you might feel overwhelmed and have started to wonder whether you have the skills required to succeed. To cope with these insecurities, you might ask other students in your class how they are finding the material. What a relief it is when they admit that they are finding the coursework difficult as well! And how anxiety-producing it is if they all claim that they find statistics easy!

According to the *control theory of self-regulation*, comparing oneself with a relevant standard allows us to maintain valued aspects of our self (Carver & Scheier, 1981, 1998). Through comparison, we can determine whether the standard we've set for ourselves is being met, and if it is not, adjust our behaviour accordingly. Let's say that as a psychology student, you consider yourself to be hard-working. The only way to know whether you are actually hard-working is to compare yourselves to others in a relevant context, in this case, other students on your psychology course. If you see that you are indeed harder working than your peers, then you can confirm your view of yourself as hard-working. If you determine that you are not actually working as hard as those around you and you still value this aspect of your self, then you might adjust your behaviour, perhaps by spending more time on your assessments or engaging more with outside reading. Either way, it is through others that the benchmark is set; how you meet that benchmark is determined by how you feel you measure up. Without the standard that others provide, 'hard-working' is meaningless.

In addition to helping us define our self-concepts, the expectations others have of us act as important guides for how we feel and behave. Higgins's (1987) *self-discrepancy theory* states that we are guided by three versions of our self: our 'actual self' (i.e., who we are currently), our 'ideal self' (i.e., who we would like to be), and our 'ought self' (i.e., who we think we should be). Although we may have some control over the former two, the latter is determined by others in our social world. For instance, let's say that you are currently a shop assistant (i.e., your actual self) but that you want to be an artist (i.e., your ideal self). However, your parents want you to become a doctor (i.e., your ought self). According to Higgins (1987), it is your 'ideal self' and your 'ought self' that motivate your behaviours (e.g., painting on your day off from work or researching medical schools). Any discrepancies that exist between these and your 'actual self' shape your feelings and behaviours. As an example, you may feel depressed about the fact that your dreams of being an artist are not being realised or feel anxious about disappointing your parents (Higgins et al., 1986). To cope with these, you might engage in *self-regulation*, where you employ strategies to reduce discrepancies (and associated discomfort) between these three selves. These might include defying your parents and going to art school or giving up painting and convincing yourself that you can find happiness in medical school. Either way, how we choose to reconcile discrepancies between our different selves have important implications for who we are.

Although both of these theories place one's self at the centre for its development, it is clear that this cannot happen without others.

Others are necessary to give meaning to our self-concepts and to set expectations for what we strive for. All of these serve to influence how we think, behave, and feel, and ultimately who we are. In the next section, we focus more specifically on how individual others shape our self.

OTHERS AS A POINT OF INDIVIDUAL COMPARISON

Individual others act as teachers for who we are. This might be through the way they treat us, what we think their perception of us is, and how we view ourselves from their perspective. Williams James (1890) wrote that 'a man has as many social selves as there are individuals who recognise him' to describe the way that our understanding of who we are is based on others' perceptions. As an example, a female professor with kids might be perceived as a scholar by her students and colleagues, but as a mother by the parents of her children's friends. The people in her life are likely to make a number of assumptions about her based on these different identities (e.g., a professor may be assumed to be intellectual and articulate while a mother may be assumed to be protective and nurturing). The female professor in this example is undoubtedly aware of the assumptions that others have about her as she navigates these two parts of her self. They are also likely to shape which attributes she emphasises (i.e., intellectual or nurturing) depending on who is around her.

Cooley (1902) coined the phrase 'the looking glass self' to describe the dependency that our self-perceptions have on our interactions with individual others. He argued that these interactions are comprised of three processes: First, we imagine how we appear to others. Second, we make inferences about the judgements that others make. Third, based on these inferences, we determine others' feelings about us. Importantly, we play an active role in these evaluations; a person wearing a jumper containing a political slogan will be aware that this will influence others' perceptions, judgements, and feelings about them – for better or for worse! The amount and type of effort we put into this process depends on how much we care about what others think. Goffman (1959) described this process as *impression management* or the way people adjust the aspects of their self to achieve a desired context-dependent impression. For example, you may not give a lot of thought to how you look when you attend your lecture but may spend a lot of time on your appearance before going on a date with someone you are hoping to impress.

According to researchers, there are several strategies we employ to manage the way others see us (Jones & Pittman, 1982). These include attempting to get others to think of us as competent (i.e., *self-promotion*), to like us (i.e., *ingratiation*), to think of us as dangerous (i.e., *intimidation*), to regard us as moral (i.e., *exemplification*), or to take pity on us (i.e., *supplication*). The strategy we use, and the extent to which we take that strategy, depends on the situation we are in, how much we care about others' impressions of us, and how much we depend on impression management to shape our sense of self. These strategies also influence our own self-concepts. Research suggests that the behaviour we've engaged in when managing others' impressions becomes internalised as part of our own self-concepts. For instance, if we spend a lot of energy on trying to keep others away through intimidation, we may start to believe that we are happier without close relationships (e.g., Schlenker et al., 1994).

Generally, the goal of impression management is to show the most positive version of who we are within the context we find ourselves in. This might mean engaging in self-promotion during a job interview or ingratiation when being introduced to our partner's parents. Perhaps to validate these representations of our self, we are prone to self-serving biases. According to the *false consensus effect*, we tend to view our own behaviour and beliefs as normal compared to the behaviour and beliefs of others (Ross et al., 1977). This idea is reinforced by our tendency to surround ourselves with people who think and behave in the same way that we do. This effect may be exacerbated by social media sites. For instance, on Twitter we might follow others with similar ideas as us, resulting in a constant stream of messages that serve to reinforce our own views and with this perpetuate our belief that we are the norm (Neubaum & Krämer, 2017). Yet the belief in our own typicality does not extend to how we think we compare to the average. Overwhelmingly, we view ourselves as better than average on most traits (Zell et al., 2020). We also tend to make *attribution errors* in that we are more likely to believe that our successes are caused by internal factors (e.g., personality traits), but our failures are caused by external ones (e.g., our environment; Ross et al., 1977). This might explain why after acing an exam we are quick to conclude that we must be very intelligent, but when we fail an exam, we blame the poor teaching we received! In this way, the presence of others and how we navigate our self around those others go beyond creating meaning for our self-concept; they are vital in helping us to maintain a positive sense of who we are.

Of course, we can't know for sure whether our interpretations of others' views are accurate or whether our impression management strategy has been successful. Rather, this is based on how we interpret the information we receive from our social world (e.g., what others say, their facial expressions, body language, etc.). Research has shown that people are surprisingly bad at understanding how their self-concepts are influenced by the situational contexts they are in, including the role that others play in shaping their attitudes and behaviours (Nisbett & Wilson, 1977). Overall, people prefer to believe that they have some control over their futures and tend to be critical of information that suggests otherwise (Thompson, 1999). Cumulatively, the research on how others shape our self-concept suggests accurate or not, we prefer to view ourselves in the best positive possible light. This begs the question: how do we maintain a positive self-image when comparing ourselves to others that are clearly better than us?

Tesser's (1988) *self-evaluation maintenance model* seeks to answer this question. Earlier in this chapter, we discussed *social comparison theory* which proposes that we define who we are by comparing ourselves to others (Festinger, 1954). According to this theory, we make *upward comparisons* (i.e., compare ourselves to those better than us) and *downward comparisons* (i.e., compare ourselves to those worse than us). While upward comparisons often result in negative self-esteem, it is also possible to feel good about ourselves because of our associations with successful others (i.e., *social reflection*). Our reaction to the presence of more successful others depends on two factors: how relevant the domain of success is to our concept of self and how secure we feel about our abilities in that domain. If the domain of success is irrelevant to us, or we feel confident about our own abilities, then we are unlikely to feel threatened by others' accomplishments. If this is the case, we may take the opportunity to bask in their reflection. Imagine you are a psychology student with a friend who is at the top of their class in history. As the domain of comparison is irrelevant (i.e., history rather than psychology), you are likely to feel successful through your association with this friend. After all, a successful friend reflects well! Likewise, if your high-achieving friend is part of your psychology course (i.e., the domain is relevant), but you are confident in your academic abilities, your friend's success may add to your self-esteem; surely having such an academically strong student on your degree programme is evidence that you chose to study in a top-notch department!

However, if the domain of success is relevant but you feel uncertain about your abilities, then your self-image may suffer. In this scenario, comparing ourselves to our colleague who manages to consistently ace their assessments might confirm our fear that we are not actually cut out for success in psychology. Yet even when faced with this perception, our proclivity towards self-serving biases means that we will still find ways to feel good about ourselves. Tesser (1988) identified four strategies that help us to maintain a positive self-image in this scenario. One is that we might exaggerate the person's abilities so that comparing yourself with them is no longer realistic. This might take the form of deciding that your successful friend is a genius whose abilities are far above those of normal people such as yourself. We also might decide to decrease the value of the domain of comparison. For example, you might assume that your social life is more active than your high-achieving friend's and that this is more important to you than high marks. You might also simply change the person you compare yourself to by focusing your attention on a peer who tends to score lower than you on their assessments. Finally, you could create distance between yourself and your friend by, for example, deciding that you don't have much in common with them or by making a concerted effort to meet other students on your course.

So far in this chapter, we have focused on the role that individual others play in shaping who we are. Whether it is through regulating our behaviour, supporting our general well-being, serving as a point of comparison, or showing us who we are, others play a vital role in shaping our self-concept. The next section, and indeed the rest of this book, will be devoted to the way groups influence who we are. We begin by outlining the features of social groups' influence and the impact these have on how we think, feel, and behave.

THE IMPORTANCE OF GROUPS

As influential as our interpersonal interactions may be, it is important to remember that they are part of a wider social context: when we interact with other people, we are also interacting as members of social groups. This is because it is not possible to separate ourselves from the groups that we are part of. Although we may think of ourselves as individual people (e.g., I'm Megan and I like to think of myself smart and kind. I also love chocolate!), these personal attributes are crossed with our membership to broad categories (e.g., I'm female, White, and an academic). Because we are representatives of our respective social groups, our interactions are group-based as much as they are interpersonal.

In view of this, our self-concept is guided by two distinct parts: our personal identity and our social identity (Tajfel & Turner, 1979). *Personal identity* refers to the attributes that make us an individual (e.g., specific competencies, personality traits, preferences, etc.), while *social identity* describes our membership to groups based on overarching categories (e.g., our gender, race, profession, etc.). In my example above, my description of myself using my name, personal attributes (e.g., smart and kind), and preferences (e.g., chocolate!) make up part of my personal identity. My description of myself as female, White, and an academic describe some of my social identities. According to Tajfel and Turner (1986), it is not possible to separate our personal self from our social groups (e.g., I cannot interact with the world *not* as female and White). Both personal and social identities influence our experiences with others and as such help determine who we are. We also strive to have positive self-concepts of both our personal and group identities, and both guide our thoughts, actions, beliefs, and behaviours (see Tajfel, 1981).

Many of us may have not thought much about how our group identity impacts on who we are (although those of us with stigmatised group identities may consider this regularly – see Chapter 5). Yet our group memberships are fundamental to our self-concept. When asking yourself 'Who am I?', you are likely to draw on multiple social groups (e.g., fans of a particular band, religious affili-ations, national identity, etc.). A *social group* can be defined as two or more individuals who perceive themselves to be members of the same social category (Turner, 1982). Groups can be distinguished between memberships based on a shared association (e.g., American) and those based on affection for other members (e.g., friendship groups; Gaffney & Mahajan, 2010). The former is known as a *com-mon-identity group* (i.e., an affiliation that is based on a shared connec-tion to an overarching category) and is based solely on category membership rather than personal relationships. For instance, if you identify as a woman, you will never know most of the people in the world who also identify as a woman! The latter is defined as a *com-mon-bond group* (i.e., an affiliation based on an attachment between group members; Prentice et al., 1994). In these groups, you are likely to have close, personal relationships with other group mem-bers. Whether you are linked by an overarching category (e.g., male) or personal connections (e.g., your work team), our social groups play integral parts in determining our self (Tajfel & Turner, 1979).

One of the most powerful influences our group membership has on our self is through norms. *Norms* are known rules or standards that guide our behaviours in different social settings. They can be *explicit* (e.g., stated rules) or *implicit* (e.g., inferred rules); both pro-vide us with a frame of reference for how to behave in different social settings. For instance, when you attend your psychology lec-ture, you know that you should not (usually!) start dancing on the tables at any point. However, at a nightclub, it may be perfectly acceptable to dance on the tables! The difference in the behaviour expected in these two settings (i.e., the norms associated with each) does not need to be explained to you; you learned them simply by living in your social world.

Norms are an important feature of groups; all societies and all groups within those societies consider certain behaviours to be stan-dard. They also demonstrate how our social and personal identities are one and the same. For example, you may be part of a football team that has strong group norms around teamwork and camarade-rie. You may also have a sales job, a role that emphasises competi-tion between colleagues. When thinking about who you are, you may describe yourself in line with the norms of each group (e.g., as a team player and as a competitor). Although these adjectives are used to describe your personal identity, they exist because of your social identities (i.e., football player and salesperson). In addition, the characteristic you are likely to take on depends on the social identity that is salient. In psychology, we use the term *salience* to describe when the context we're in results in one identity standing out more than another. When you are on the football pitch, your identity as a football player likely becomes salient (and with that you may adopt the norm of working as a team). When you are on the sales floor, it is your identity as a salesperson that becomes salient (and you may act in line with the norm of being competitive). Therefore, the salience of a social identity helps determine the norms that will guide your behaviour in that setting.

BOX 2.1   REAL-WORLD APPLICATION – NORMS AND COVID-19

As the United Kingdom prepared for their first national lockdown in March 2020 to curb the spread of COVID-19, newspapers around the country were reporting that everyday necessities, such as toilet paper, were in increasingly short supply at supermarkets. Often these news stories were accompanied by photographs of empty shelves.

The result of this narrative was that of a self-fulfilling prophecy. Initially, these stories were inspired by a small minority of the population who were purchasing large amounts of products. But before long more people started picking up an extra roll or two, eventually leading to a shortage in the supply chain.

Why did this happen? One answer lies in the power of norms. As we've discussed throughout this chapter, people look to others for guidance on how to behave. This is especially true in times of ambiguity; there is little doubt that the start of a global pandemic is an ambiguous situation! Hence, the media's constant images of empty aisles sent the message that buying toilet paper is what people are doing to prepare. As this norm became established, people began to feel that this was something they should also be doing to prepare (Ntontis et al., 2022). Before we knew it, everyone was buying toilet roll!

In addition to guiding our behaviour, our social identities shape our attitudes and beliefs. When thinking about different social groups (e.g., a profession, a religion), we tend to associate them with certain characteristics (e.g., what they look like, how they behave, what they think, etc.; Hogg & Smith, 2007). For instance, you might hear about someone who works on a construction site and assume that they are White, male, physically strong, and okay with the use of crass language. Although none of these assumptions about the person may be true, they make up the general set of attributes that people tend to associate with that group (see Chapter 5 for an in-depth discussion of stereotypes). Categorising one's self and others in line with their group membership is known as *depersonalisation* (Turner et al., 1987). When one's social identity is salient, this process can result in individuals conforming their attitudes and beliefs to those of the group (e.g., I am likely to agree with a change to tax laws if I identify with the political party making that change, rather than based on the proposal itself.). People are also more persuaded to adjust their attitudes and beliefs when an argument is put forward by members of their own social group compared to members of groups that they are not a part of (see Hogg & Smith, 2007).

In this way, our social identities provide parameters for which our attitudes and beliefs evolve. However, it is not just our alignment with our group that is important for this aspect of our self but our position within the groups we are a part of. For each of our social identities, we occupy a *social role* – that is, the set of behaviours that individuals occupying specific positions in the group are expected to perform. In your friendship group, for example, you may notice that one person tends to take on the organising for social events, while another is the one that group members go to for support. Of these social roles, the most influential is the group *prototype* – the group member who embodies all the traits that define the group. Importantly, prototypical group members do not represent the average of the group's traits, but rather are an exemplar of the group's ideal (Hogg & Smith, 2007). In sports teams, for example, it is often the person who exemplifies the team's goals and values who emerges as the team captain. When a social identity is salient, group members tend to look to prototypical members for guidance on how to think, look, act, and feel. This helps to explain why these members tend to emerge as the leaders of the group and are afforded more status than non-prototypical members (Steffens et al., 2020).

The social roles we occupy within our groups are an important part of who we are. This point was initially demonstrated by the classic 'Boys' Camp' studies, which were conducted between 1949 and 1954. As the name suggests, these were field studies that took place in American Summer camps. Using typical camp activities (e.g., tug of war, baseball games), the researchers manipulated competition between groups of boys to explore how relationships within the group (i.e., *intragroup dynamics*) are impacted by the presence of a competing group (i.e., *intergroup dynamics*; Sherif & Sherif, 1969). Each study had three phases: In phase one, the boys met each other and began to establish friendship groups. It was at this point that the experimenters observed how naturally group norms and social roles emerged. In phase two, the groups were pitted against each other in a series of activities in which they competed for valued prizes. In phase three, the experimenters orchestrated opportunities for positive contact between group members (e.g., movie nights, setting up camp) to understand the conditions under which the intergroup hostility evoked by intergroup competition in phase two might be reduced (Sherif & Sherif, 1969).

The results of these studies demonstrate the interplay between personal identity and social identity. Once the boys were split into separate groups and encouraged to compete, the roles and norms established during phase one shifted dramatically; social roles were adjusted so that new prototypes who reflected the group's new goals (e.g., the desire to win) emerged as the leader. In this case, new norms around acting 'tough' were adhered to and enforced (see Platow & Hunter, 2017). The researchers also noted that the influence of the group on the boys' attitudes and beliefs was so strong that even before any competition was introduced, group members expressed disdain for the other group. This observation demonstrates the power that simply being part of a group has for how we think and behave. Finally, as the group became increasingly fixated on winning, the boys' identification with their respective groups became so strong that their groups' goals became synonymous with their personal goals (Sherif & Sherif, 1969).

Two key lessons about the relationship between the group and the self can be taken from these studies. The first is that our group's dynamics and structure are internalised as part of our self-concept. Group norms, group goals, and our social role within the group guide our individual behaviour, drive our personal goals, and shape our attitudes. In this way, Sherif and Sherif (1969) were able to demonstrate how our group identity *is* our personal identity. The second lesson is that these dynamics are not fixed but fluctuate as our social world changes. For example, the behaviour, goals, and attitudes of a person who has just become a parent may be noticeably different than the behaviour, goals, and the attitudes they held in the years before when they did not have this responsibility. Because our self is intertwined with our membership to groups, as our social identities evolve, so does who we are.

However, it is not the case that we blindly go along with any change that occurs within our group. Rather, whether changes are adopted into aspects of one's self-concept depends on whether these changes are perceived to be in line with perceptions of the group's core aims. If the change imposed is perceived as undermining the group's identity, then group members may choose to create a new group or to join a different group entirely (Sani, 2008). This is known as a *schism*. One example of a schism is the exodus of thousands of Church of England members (including hundreds of clergymen) following the decision to permit women as priests (Sani & Reicher, 2000). For these members, the ordination of women corrupted the group's identity to such an extent that they felt their best option was to break away from the group entirely (Sani, 2008). Schisms have also been observed through the language used to discuss the group's aims. Using Facebook posts with the #OccupyWallStreet, Smith and colleagues (2015) demonstrated how subgroups emerged within the Occupy movement that were based on members' divergent beliefs about how best to address financial injustices.

One factor that determines how group members might respond to unwelcome changes within the group is the fear of marginalisation. If members trust that their voice, however dissenting, will still be heard and respected, they may be less likely to join a schism. After all, given how important our group memberships are to our basic psychological functioning (Baumeister & Leary, 1995), the decision to leave an important social group is not an easy one (see the earlier discussion about the dissolution of social relationships). Despite this, if members suspect they will be marginalised, then joining a schism may feel like the best option (Sani, 2008). Research suggests that group members are wise to want to avoid being marginalised. *Marginal group members* are considered deviants, either because they are seen to have strayed too far from the group's prototype or because they also identify with a competing group. These members are generally disliked and may be judged especially harshly (Reese et al., 2013). Ironically, when marginal members leave a group, they tend to become more accepted and their ideas given more consideration than if they had stayed (Curşeu et al., 2012). This change in attitude can be explained by the threat that marginal group members pose to the group's identity. When that threat is present (because marginal members are part of the group), these members are viewed negatively. However, when this threat is removed (because these members leave the group), they tend to be viewed more positively (Jetten & Hornsey, 2014).

As this section demonstrates, the core of who we are is determined by our membership to groups. When our group membership is salient, group norms and our role within the group drive our attitudes and beliefs. As we have seen, these are so intertwined that our personal and social identities cannot be separated: In short, we are the groups that we belong to. In the next section, we discuss what is arguably one of the most influential groups that help determine our self: our culture.

CULTURAL DIFFERENCES IN SELF-CONCEPT

After Olympic diver Wu Minxia won gold for China in the 2012 London Olympics, it was revealed that her parents had been withholding information from her: Her grandparents had died the year before and her mother had been battling cancer for 8 years. The reason? They did not want to distract her from her training. When asked about their decision, Wu's father is quoted as saying that "we long ago realised that our daughter doesn't belong to us completely" (Rosenfield, 2012). Considering that children demonstrating athletic potential are often removed from their homes and placed in government-run sporting schools, we can presume that Wu's father perceives his daughter as belonging, at least in part, to China.

Wu's story garnered criticism around the world (including in China), but her parents' actions seemed particularly alien to people in the West. The reason for this may be partly explained by cultural differences that exist between China and Western countries (e.g., the United Kingdom, the United States, Australia). Just as social norms vary across our different social groups and contexts, they also vary across cultures. Although notably difficult to define, *culture* can be described as the socially shared values, beliefs, and expectations of a group of people (Betancourt & Flynn, 2009). China is an example of a *collectivist culture* because of their emphasis on loyalty to the group and the individual's role in benefitting the collective good. This helps to explain why Wu's parents seemed to emphasise her importance to China over their needs as a family. Western countries, on the other hand, are examples of *individualistic cultures* which value individual uniqueness, choice, and a separation from others. This helps to explain why the decision that Wu's parents made to sacrifice their family life to contribute towards China's Olympic ambitions seemed particularly strange to people from individualistic countries.

Whether a culture is individualist or collectivist helps determine the *self-construal* of its inhabitants. Coined by Markus and Kitayama (1991), self-construal describes how individuals see and create meaning for their self in relation to others. According to this perspective, self-construal is a trait that is characterised by independence and interdependence. Those with an independent self-construal see others in terms of how they benefit the self; in this way, others are used to confirm their own uniqueness. Those with an interdependent self-construal define who they are through their relationships with others, place importance on how they benefit those others, and prize the ability to fit in with the crowd (Markus & Kitayama, 1991). While our self-construal may veer towards one extreme or the other, the values that we develop will be influenced by the cultural context we find ourselves in (with individualistic cultures valuing independence and collectivist cultures valuing interdependence; Cross et al., 2011).

However, differences between cultures are more complex than binary notions of individualism/independence and collectivism/interdependence. Interdependence itself varies depending on whether relationships are defined as those that are interpersonal or those that are group-based (i.e., *relational self-construal*; Cross et al., 2011). Cultures can also vary along a *looseness–tightness dimension* with regard to how strictly social norms are expected to be adhered to and the degree of sanctions imposed on those who deviate from them (Gelfand et al., 2006). *Power distance* refers to the level of acceptance around unequal distributions of power within a society (Hofstede, 1980), while *uncertainty avoidance* describes the extent to which ambiguity in society is limited through tradition and religion (Hofstede, 2001). Cultures are not necessarily on one extreme or the other, but generally fall somewhere along these continuums. Given that people are also part of multiple groups within their respective cultures that also impact on their self, the specific influence of culture on who we are is far from straightforward.

Still, there is little doubt that our culture plays an important role in shaping who we are. Even our basic cognitive processes are impacted by our culture (Nisbett & Masuda, 2003). In a demonstration of the way that culture influences our causal attributions, researchers found that when asked to describe a sporting event, American newspapers tended to focus on the traits and abilities of the individual players (i.e., internal attributions), while Chinese newspapers focused more on the situation itself (i.e., external attributions; Lee et al., 1996). These differences extend to how we categorise information. Researchers showed both Chinese and American participants a picture of a cow, a chicken, and some grass, and asked them to group two of the pictures together. American participants grouped the cow and the chicken together based on the logic that they are both animals, while Chinese participants paired the cow with grass based on the logic that cows eat grass (Chiu, 1972). These differences in thinking may also extend to problem-solving ability with those from individualistic cultures generally having more success with rule-based problems and those from collectivist cultures generally having more success with context-based problems (Arieli & Sagiv, 2018). Nisbett and Masuda (2003) argue that these differences might be explained by the role of networking in these cultures. Because fitting in and getting along with the group are emphasised in collectivist cultures compared to individualistic cultures, the former may be more sensitive to social cues given off by the situation's context.

How we behave is also influenced by our culture. For instance, people in collectivist cultures tend to manage their emotions by modelling others in their immediate environment (Liddell & Williams, 2019). People from these cultures also tend to be less extraverted, the personality trait characterised by being outgoing, loud, and sociable (McCrae & Terracciano, 2005) and may be more likely to consider their relationships with others when making career decisions compared to those from individualistic cultures (Guan et al., 2015). Individuals from cultures that rank high (as opposed to low) on power distance tend to value submission, particularly when interacting with someone of higher status (Matsumoto, 2007), while people from tighter (as opposed to looser) cultures engage in more social comparisons (Baldwin & Mussweiler, 2018). Finally, those from cultures that are high (vs. low) on avoiding uncertainty often score higher on traits associated with neuroticism (e.g., higher levels of emotional distress and mood swings; Allik & McCrae, 2004). According to Sng and colleagues (2018), even subtle aspects of our culture's environment influence our behaviour. For instance, populations with higher densities may be less aggressive, while those with high rates of genetic relatedness (i.e., lots of family around) may be more helpful.

This section barely scratches the surface in reviewing the rich literature in cultural psychology. However, what is clear is that the culture in which we grow up and live is a key determinant of our self. Yet unlike other social groups whose influence might change based on its salience within a given context, everyone in our social world, irrespective of their belonging to other social groups, generally shares the same overarching culture. Hence, our culture is so embedded within us that we might barely notice its impact on who we are. Indeed, it may not be until we are experiencing a culture that is different to our own that we realise just how dependent we are on the meaning our culture provides for guiding how to think, feel, and behave. In this way, our culture is a prime example of how dependent we are on others in our social world for every aspect of who we are: our thoughts, values, beliefs, and behaviour all depend on them. Just as it is impossible to imagine a society without culture, it is impossible to consider the self without others.

CONCLUSION

Others influence who we are in a multitude of ways and on both interpersonal and group levels. As we have seen, everything from the clothes we decide to wear each day to our basic psychological functioning is driven by our relationships to others and the standards they set. As social animals, human beings depend on each other not only to know how to think and act but for basic survival. In the chapters that follow, we will be delving deeper into the premise that our self is driven by our social relationships by focusing specifically on the inextricable link between our self and our social identities. In doing so, we will not only explore further how others guide our self but will show how our identification to our social groups can predicate the evolution of our society. Now that we understand that the self is a social relationship, we can consider how this relationship is relevant to every aspect of our social world.

CHAPTER SUMMARY

- Feeling a sense of belonging is necessary to maintain normal psychological functioning.
- Ostracism is used to regulate behaviour. The experience of ostracism affects our thoughts, feelings, and behaviours.
- The meaning of our self-concepts depends on others in our social world.
- We are prone to biases in our thinking that place as in a positive light, and we often align our thinking to confirm this bias.
- Our personal identity is intertwined with our group memberships. Group norms, goals, and the role we play in our groups drive our thoughts, feelings, and behaviours.
- Cultures differ on a variety of dimensions that guide our thoughts, values, beliefs, and behaviours .

WANT TO KNOW MORE?

Recommended Reading:
- Aronson, E. (2018). *The social animal*. Worth Publishers
- Heine, S. J. (2020). *Cultural psychology*. W. W. Norton & Company

REFERENCES

Allik, J., & McCrae, R. R. (2004). Toward a geography of personality traits: Patterns of profiles across 36 cultures. *Journal of Cross-Cultural Psychology, 34,* 13–28. https://doi.org/10.1177/0022022103260382

Arieli, S., & Sagiv, L. (2018). Culture and problem-solving: Congruency between the cultural mindset of individualism versus collectivism and problem type. *Journal of Experimental Psychology: General, 147*(6), 789–814. https://doi.org/10.1037/xge0000444

Baldwin, M., & Mussweiler, T. (2018). The culture of social comparison. *Proceedings of the National Academy of Sciences, 115*(39). https://doi.org/10.1073/pnas.1721555115

Baumeister, R. F., & Leary, M. R. (1995). The need to belong: Desire for interpersonal attachments as a fundamental human motivation. *Psychological Bulletin, 117*(3), 497–529. http://doi.org/10.1037/0033-2909.117.3.497

Baumeister, R. F., Twenge, J. M., & Nuss, C. K. (2002). Effects of social exclusion on cognitive processes: Anticipated aloneness reduces intelligent thought. *Journal of Personality and Social Psychology, 83*(4), 817. https://doi.org/10.1037/0022-3514.83.4.817

Betancourt, H., & Flynn, P. M. (2009). The psychology of health: Physical health and the role of culture and behavior. In F. A. Villarruel, G. Carlo, J. M. Grau, M. Azmitia, N. J. Cabrera, & T. J. Chahin (Eds.), *Handbook of U.S. Latino psychology: Developmental and community-based perspectives* (pp. 347–361). Sage Publications, Inc

Broncano-Berrocal, F., & Carter, J. A. (2020). *The philosophy of group polarization.* Routledge

Carver, C. S., & Scheier, M. F. (1981). *Attention and self-regulation: A control-theory approach to human behavior.* Springer-Verlag.

Carver, C. S., & Scheier, M. F. (1998). *On the self-regulation of behavior.* Cambridge University Press

Chiu, L. H. (1972). A cross-cultural comparison of cognitive styles in Chinese and American children. *International Journal of Psychology, 7*(4), 235–242. https://doi.org/10.1080/00207597208246604

Cohen, S., Doyle, W. J., Skoner, D. P., Rabin, B. S., & Gwaltney, J. M. (1997). Social ties and susceptibility to the common cold. *JAMA, 277*(24), 1940–1944. http://doi.org/10.1001/jama.1997.03540480040036

Cooley, C. H. (1902). Looking-glass self. In O'Brien (Ed.), *The production of reality: Essays and readings on social interaction* (Vol. 6, pp. 126–128). Sage

Cross, S. E., Hardin, E. E., & Gercek-Swing, B. (2011). The what, how, why, and where of self-construal. *Personality and Social Psychology Review, 15*(2), 142–179. https://doi.org/10.1177/1088868310373752

Curşeu, P. L., Schruijer, S. G., & Boroş, S. (2012). Socially rejected while cognitively successful? The impact of minority dissent on groups' cognitive complexity. *British Journal of Social Psychology, 51*(4), 570–582. https://doi.org/10.1111/j.2044-8309.2011.02023.x

Eisenberger, N. I., Lieberman, M. D., & Williams, K. D. (2003). Does rejection hurt? An fMRI study of social exclusion. *Science, 302*(5643), 290–292. http://doi.org/10.1126/science.1089134

Festinger, L. (1954). A theory of social comparison processes. *Human Relations, 7*(2), 117–140. https://doi.org/10.1177/001872675400700202

Gaffney, A., & Mahajan, N. (2010). Common-identity/common-bond groups. In J. M. Levine, & M. A. Hogg (Eds.), *Encyclopedia of group processes & intergroup relations* (pp. 118–119). Sage Publications, Inc., https://www.doi.org/10.4135/9781412972017.n37

Gelfand, M. J., Nishii, L. H., & Raver, J. L. (2006). On the nature and importance of cultural tightness-looseness. *Journal of Applied Psychology, 91*(6), 1225. https://doi.org/10.1037/0021-9010.91.6.1225

Goffman, E. (1959). *The presentation of self in everyday life.* Allen Lane The Penguin Press.

Gonsalkorale, K., & Williams, K. D. (2007). The KKK won't let me play: Ostracism even by a despised outgroup hurts. *European Journal of Social Psychology, 37*(6), 1176–1186. https://doi.org/10.1002/ejsp.392

Greenaway, K. H., Cruwys, T., Haslam, S. A., & Jetten, J. (2016). Social identities promote well-being because they satisfy global psychological needs. *European Journal of Social Psychology, 46*(3), 294–307. http://doi.org/10.1002/ejsp.2169

Guan, Y., Chen, S. X., Levin, N., Bond, M. H., Luo, N., Xu, J., … Han, X. (2015). Differences in career decision-making profiles between American and Chinese university students: The relative strength of mediating mechanisms across cultures. *Journal of Cross-Cultural Psychology, 46*(6), 856–872. https://doi.org/10.1177/0022022115585874

Higgins, E. T. (1987). Self-discrepancy: A theory relating self and affect. *Psychological Review, 94*(3), 319–340. https://doi.org/10.1037/0033-295X.94.3.319

Higgins, E. T., Bond, R. N., Klein, R., & Strauman, T. (1986). Self-discrepancies and emotional vulnerability: How magnitude, accessibility, and type of discrepancy influence affect. *Journal of Personality and Social Psychology, 51*(1), 5–15. https://doi.org/10.1037/0022-3514.51.1.5

Hofstede, G. (1980). *Culture's consequences: International differences in work-related values.* Sage

Hofstede, G. (2001). *Culture's consequences: Comparing values, behaviors, institutions, and organizations across nations* (2nd Ed., pp. 79–123). Sage

Hogg, M. A., & Smith, J. R. (2007). Attitudes in social context: A social identity perspective. *European Review of Social Psychology, 18*(1), 89–131. https://doi.org/10.1080/10463280701592070

Holt-Lunstad, J., Robles, T. F., & Sbarra, D. A. (2017). Advancing social connection as a public health priority in the United States. *American Psychologist, 72*(6), 517. https://doi.org/10.1037/amp0000103

James, W. (1890). *The principles of psychology* (Vol. 1). Henry Holt and Company

Jetten, J., & Hornsey, M. J. (2014). Deviance and dissent in groups. *Annual Review of Psychology, 65*, 461–485. https://doi.org/10.1146/annurev-psych-010213-115151

Jones, J. M., & Jetten, J. (2011). Recovering from strain and enduring pain: Multiple group memberships promote resilience in the face of physical challenges. *Social Psychological and Personality Science, 2*(3), 239–244. https://doi.org/10.1177/1948550610386806

Jones, E. E., & Pittman, T. (1982). Toward a general theory of strategic self-presentation. In J. Suls (Ed.), *Psychological perspectives on the self* (Vol. 1, pp. 231–262). Erlbaum.

Kawakami, N., & Yoshida, F. (2015). How do implicit effects of subliminal mere exposure become explicit? Mediating effects of social interaction. *Social Influence, 10*(1), 43–54. https://doi.org/10.1080/15534510.2014.901245

Lee, F., Hallahan, M., & Herzog, T. (1996). Explaining real-life events: How culture and domain shape attributions. *Personality and Social Psychology Bulletin, 22*(7), 732–741. https://doi.org/10.1177/0146167296227007

Liddell, B. J., & Williams, E. N. (2019). Cultural differences in interpersonal emotion regulation. *Frontiers in Psychology, 10*, 999. https://doi.org/10.3389/fpsyg.2019.00999

Markus, H. R., & Kitayama, S. (1991). Culture and the self: Implications for cognition, emotion, and motivation. *Psychological Review, 98*(2), 224–253. https://doi.org/10.1037/0033-295X.98.2.224

Matsumoto, D. (2007). Individual and cultural differences in status differentiation: The status differentiation scale. *Journal of Cross-Cultural Psychology, 38*, 413–431. https://doi.org/10.1177/0022022107302311

McCrae, R. R., Terracciano, A., & Personality Profiles of Cultures Project. (2005). Personality profiles of cultures: Aggregate personality traits. *Journal of Personality and Social Psychology, 89*(3), 407–425. https://doi.org/10.1037/0022-3514.89.3.407

Moscovici, S., & Zavalloni, M. (1969). The group as a polarizer of attitudes. *Journal of Personality and Social Psychology, 12*(2), 125–135. https://doi.org/10.1037/h0027568

Neubaum, G., & Krämer, N. C. (2017). Monitoring the opinion of the crowd: Psychological mechanisms underlying public opinion perceptions on social media. *Media Psychology, 20*(3), 502–531. https://doi.org/10.1080/15213269.2016.1211539

Nisbett, R. E., & Masuda, T. (2003). Culture and point of view. *Proceedings of the National Academy of Sciences, 100*(19), 11163–11170. https://doi.org/10.1073/pnas.1934527100

Nisbett, R. E., & Wilson, T. D. (1977). Telling more than we can know: Verbal reports on mental processes. *Psychological Review, 84*(3), 231. https://doi.org/10.1037/0033-295X.84.3.231

Nowak, M., & Highfield, R. (2011). *Supercooperators: Altruism, evolution, and why we need each other to succeed.* Simon and Schuster

Ntontis, E., Vestergren, S., Saavedra, P., Neville, F., Jurstakova, K., Cocking, C., et al. (2022). Is it really "panic buying"? Public perceptions and experiences of extra buying at the onset of the COVID-19 pandemic. *PLoS One, 17*(2), e0264618

Platow, M. J., & Hunter, J. A. (2017). Intergroup relations and conflict: Revisiting Sherif's boys' camp studies. In J. R. Smith, & S. A. Haslam (Eds.), *Social psychology: Revisiting the classic studies* (2nd Ed., pp. 146–164). Sage

Prentice, D. A., Miller, D. T., & Lightdale, J. R. (1994). Asymmetries in attachments to groups and to their members: Distinguishing between common-identity and common-bond groups. *Personality and Social Psychology Bulletin, 20*(5), 484–493. https://doi.org/10.1177/0146167294205005

Reese, G., Steffens, M. C., & Jonas, K. J. (2013). When black sheep make us think: Information processing and devaluation of in-and outgroup norm deviants. *Social Cognition, 31*(4), 482–503. https://doi.org/10.1521/soco_2012_1005

Rosenfield (2012). https://olympics.time.com/2012/08/03/wu-minxia-chinese-divers-parents-hid-family-illness-deaths-from-her/

Ross, L., Greene, D., & House, P. (1977). The "false consensus effect": An egocentric bias in social perception and attribution processes. *Journal of Experimental Social Psychology, 13*(3), 279–301. https://doi.org/10.1016/0022-1031(77)90049-X

Sani, F. (2008). Schism in groups: A social psychological account. *Social and Personality Psychology Compass, 2*(2), 718–732. https://doi.org/10.1111/j.1751-9004.2007.00073.x

Sani, F., & Reicher, S. (2000). Contested identities and schisms in groups: Opposing the ordination of women as priests in the Church of England. *British Journal of Social Psychology, 39*(1), 95–112. https://doi.org/10.1348/014466600164354

Schlenker, B. R., Dlugolecki, D. W., & Doherty, K. J. (1994). The impact of self-presentations on self-appraisals and behaviors: The power of public commitment. *Personality and Social Psychology Bulletin, 20*, 20–33. https://doi.org/10.1177/0146167294201002

Sherif, M., & Sherif, C. W. (1969). *Social psychology.* Harper & Row.

Smith, L. G., Gavin, J., & Sharp, E. (2015). Social identity formation during the emergence of the occupy movement. *European Journal of Social Psychology, 45*(7), 818–832. http://doi.org/10.1002/ejsp.2150

Sng, O., Neuberg, S. L., Varnum, M. E., & Kenrick, D. T. (2018). The behavioral ecology of cultural psychological variation. *Psychological Review, 125*(5), 714–743. https://doi.org/10.1037/rev0000104

Steffens, N. K., Cruwys, T., Haslam, C., Jetten, J., & Haslam, S. A. (2016). Social group memberships in retirement are associated with reduced risk of premature death: Evidence from a longitudinal cohort study. *BMJ Open, 6*(2). http://doi.org/10.1136/bmjopen-2015-010164

Steffens, N. K., Munt, K. A., van Knippenberg, D., Platow, M. J., & Haslam, S. A. (2020). Advancing the social identity theory of leadership: A meta-analytic review of leader group prototypicality. *Organizational Psychology Review, 11*(1), 35–72. https://doi.org/10.1177/2041386620962569

Suls, J., Wheeler, L. (2000). A selective history of classic and neo-social comparison theory. In J. Suls & L. Wheeler (Eds.) *Handbook of social comparison. The springer series in social clinical psychology*. Springer. https://doi.org/10.1007/978-1-4615-4237-7_1

Tajfel, H. (1981). *Human groups and social categories: Studies in social psychology*. Cambridge University Press

Tajfel, H. & Turner, J. C. (1979). An integrative theory of intergroup conflict. In W. Austin & S. Worchel (Eds.), *The social psychology of intergroup relations* (pp. 33–48). Brooks/Cole.

Tajfel, H., & Turner, J. C. (1986). The social identity theory of intergroup behavior. In S. Worchel & W. Austin (Eds.), *Psychology of intergroup relations* (pp. 7–24). Nelson Hall.

Tesser, A. (1988). Toward a self-evaluation maintenance model of social behavior. *Advances in Experimental Social Psychology, 21*, 181–227. https://doi.org/10.1016/S0065-2601(08)60227-0

Thompson, S. C. (1999). Illusions of control: How we overestimate our personal influence. *Current Directions in Psychological Science, 8*(6), 187–190. http://doi.org/10.1111/1467-8721.00044

Turner, J. C. (1982). Towards a redefinition of the social group. In H. Tajfel (Ed.), *Social identity and intergroup relations* (pp. 15–40). Cambridge University Press.

Turner, J. C., Hogg, M. A., Oakes, P. J., Reicher, S. D., & Wetherell, M. S. (1987). *Rediscovering the social group: A self-categorisation theory*. Blackwell

Wesselmann, E. D., Ren, D., & Williams, K. D. (2015). Motivations for responses to ostracism. *Frontiers in Psychology, 6*, 40. https://doi.org/10.3389/fpsyg.2015.00040

Williams, K. D. (2009). Ostracism: Effects of being excluded and ignored. In M. Zanna (Ed.), *Advances in experimental social psychology* (pp. 275–314). Academic Press

Zell, E., Strickhouser, J. E., Sedikides, C., & Alicke, M. D. (2020). The better-than-average effect in comparative self-evaluation: A comprehensive review and meta-analysis. *Psychological Bulletin, 146*(2), 118. http://doi.org/10.1037/bul0000218

the other. The boys were then taken into cubicles and told the outcome of their responses. All were given the same, meaningless, group membership: boys who estimated the number of dots were classified as under-estimators (rather than over-estimators) and those who had given their preferences of the paintings were 'Klee favouring' (rather than 'Kandinsky favouring'; Tajfel et al., 1971).

Following this, the boys were given a booklet of matrices and asked to assign rewards to members of their own group (other under-estimators or other Klee favourers) and to members of the other group (over-estimators or Wassily favourers; Tajfel et al., 1971). The rewards had little value; each point equated to 0.1 of a penny. Importantly, the boys knew nothing about the people they were assigning the points to other than that their answers in the task had (supposedly) made them a fellow member of the *in-group* (i.e., the group that one is a part of) or a member of the *out-group* (i.e., a group that one is not a part of). On the left of the matrix, points for both groups were low, but the distribution meant that the in-group member would receive the most points relative to the out-group member (e.g., seven points for the in-group member as opposed to one point for the out-group member). On the right, the out-group would receive more points, but both groups would receive the highest possible number of points (e.g., 19 points as opposed to 25 points). In the middle of the matrices, point allocation was equal for both group members (Tajfel et al., 1971).

Across the minimal group studies, the boys consistently chose a point distribution that was somewhere in between the left and the middle (i.e., maximum gain for the in-group relative to the out-group and fairness). Instead of choosing a strategy that would maximise the number of points that their group members would receive, the boys were willing to sacrifice points when doing so meant the in-group member would receive more than the out-group member (Tajfel et al., 1971). In other words, it was more important to do better than the out-group than it was to do well. This was surprising because it demonstrated that all the factors that had previously been assumed to be essential for intergroup discrimination (e.g., a history of conflict, personal animosity, negative interdependence, etc.) were not needed: even when group membership was completely random and meaningless, the boys preferred their own group at the expense of the group they were not a part of (Tajfel et al., 1971).

What did these findings suggest about people and groups? Explanations such as individual self-interest and personal economic gain were ruled out because the task required the boys to assign points to anonymous group members but never to themselves. Follow-up studies showed that this pattern could also not be attributed to assumptions about similarity; people assigned more points to an in-group member than someone known to have similar interests (Billig & Tajfel, 1973). In other studies, the pattern found in the minimal group paradigm extended to evaluations of groups; when participants were asked about their thoughts on their fellow in-group member, they used more positive attributes than they did when asked to describe the out-group member (Doise et al., 1972). Hence, it seemed that Tafjel had found his answer: simply belonging to a group, even in the absence of any meaning at all, is enough to favour one's own group at the expense of another.

These findings became the basis for social identity theory (Tajfel & Turner, 1979). Tajfel and his colleagues theorised that rather than focusing on factors such as competition or historical animosities, understanding group processes depends on understanding social identity (Tajfel, 1972). As explained in Chapter 2, we are all members of social groups (e.g., based on gender, race, nationality, etc.), and these social identities make up who we are. Social identity theory takes this idea further by arguing that because our social identity is inextricably linked with our personal identity, we seek to define our social groups in distinct and positive ways. By doing this, we are also defining our *self* in distinct and positive ways. This process depends on having a relevant group of comparison. For instance, a British person is unable to define their British identity without another nationality to compare it to. You could not, for instance, know what it means to be British by comparing the group to people who like concerts; this group does not offer a relevant means of comparison. You can, however, understand what it means to be British by comparing this group to the French or any other national group. According to Tajfel (1972), differentiating our own group from others is what validates our identity and gives it its meaning.

Once we have identified with our group and compared it to relevant others, we seek to view our group positively. Depending on the group of comparison, this can be achieved in different ways.

In an example based on stereotypes, a British person may feel that their British identity means they are hard-working when comparing their group to the French, but that they are polite when comparing their group to the Germans. Social identity theory argues that whatever national group the British person uses, the result will be that their group is not only distinct from the out-group but also more positive than them. The tendency to view our own group more positively than other groups is known as *in-group bias*. This phenomenon helps to explain why participants in the minimal group studies favoured their own group, even in the absence of any meaning. In fact, evidence of in-group bias has been found in children as young as 3 years old, suggesting that humans may have evolved to use even the most seemingly insignificant markers of group membership to guide their social preferences (Richter et al., 2016).

In sum, social identity theory lays out three stages and makes one assumption when people differentiate themselves into groups (Tajfel & Turner, 1979). First, we identity with the social group that is salient within a given context. Second, we validate the meaning of this social identity by comparing our group to other groups based on a shared superordinate dimension (e.g., Manchester United fans might compare themselves to Liverpool fans on the basis that both love football). This process is called *social comparison*. Then, assuming we want to view ourselves, and by extension our groups, positively (i.e., we seek to achieve *positive distinctiveness*), we differentiate our group from other groups in positive ways (i.e., *social differentiation*). Through these stages and the assumption of positive distinctiveness, social identity theory helps to explain the psychological processes behind the integration of our group identity into our self. In the next section, we will discuss how these processes play out in the social world in which we live.

POSITIVE DISTINCTIVENESS IN AN UNEQUAL WORLD

While the differentiation process helps explain why even random and meaningless groups are important to our self-concept, it raises an important question: If our aim is to distinguish our social identities from others in positive ways, how do we achieve this when we are part of groups that are stigmatised or negatively defined? That is, in a world full of inequalities, how do those of us with social identities that are low in status and power positively differentiate our group from comparison groups that high are in status and power?

Social identity theory proposes that in this situation, we still seek positive distinctiveness for our groups, but how we achieve this depends on two factors. The first is the *permeability* of group boundaries, that is, whether it's possible to change groups. If boundaries between our low-status group and the relevant high-status group are permeable, then we will distance ourselves from our group and seek to define ourselves more as an individual than as a group member. This is the first step towards leaving our low-status group to join the group of higher status. Take, for example, someone who grew up in working-class neighbourhood but who believes that access to the middle class is not only desirable but also possible. Their response may be to start emulating the middle class (perhaps by altering their accent or way of dress) and to work towards achieving access to this group, for instance by studying for a university degree. Because the person believed that access to the higher status group (e.g., the middle class) from the lower status group (e.g., the working class) is possible (i.e., group boundaries are permeable), they positively distinguish themselves by taking steps towards joining the group they perceive as more desirable.

If boundaries are perceived as impermeable, then the quest for positive distinctiveness will depend on a second factor: *legitimacy* (or stability). Legitimacy refers to the degree to which groups perceive the status and power differences between them as just and fair (Hornsey et al., 2003). There are several reasons why low-status group members might not question their position, not least because they may have internalised the stigma attached to their group (see Chapter 5). Low-status groups who do not see their position as contestable engage in *social creativity* to achieve positive distinctiveness: this involves increasing their identification with their group and focusing on aspects of that identity that they perceive to be more positive than that of the relevant high-status out-group. Let's go back to our example of a person who thinks of themselves as working class. This time, the person does not believe it is possible to join the middle class (i.e., boundaries are perceived to be impermeable), and they have not questioned the lower status position they find their group in (i.e., status differences are perceived to be legitimate). In this situation, the person might engage in social creativity by embracing their working-class identity and emphasising the parts of this identity that they feel positively distinguish themselves from the middle class (e.g., the importance of community within their neighbourhood). They might also change their group of comparison (e.g., by focusing on how they are better off than groups that are less advantaged than their own), or they might even redefine the way they conceptualise their group (e.g., drawing on the virtue of hard work and struggle; Reicher et al., 2010). By being creative about what they can feel good about during the social comparison process, members of negatively defined groups are able to maintain a sense of positive distinctiveness, despite their lower status in broader society.

One example of how strategies to gain positive distinctiveness are impacted by the interplay between permeability and legitimacy is the dynamic between smokers and non-smokers. Due to the increasing stigma around smoking in recent decades, smokers are arguably the low-status group compared to non-smokers. Smokers know the effects of cigarettes on both their health and the health of others and are thus unlikely to question the legitimacy of their position (for instance, by querying why they must smoke outside when it's raining). Those who perceive that access to the high-status, non-smoking out-group as permeable (e.g., they believe they can quit) are likely to at least make attempts to join this group. However, those who view group boundaries as impermeable (e.g., because they don't want to quit or don't believe that quitting is possible) may engage in social creativity instead. This might involve distinguishing themselves from non-smokers by emphasising positive attributes they feel are unique to their group (e.g., the social aspects of smoking or the laid-back attitude they might have towards risk). Hence, being in a group low in status does not prevent us from viewing our group in positive and distinct ways; it's just that we employ different strategies to gain this positive distinctiveness depending on our view of the boundaries and status relations that exist between those groups.

Of course, it is also possible for low-status group members to perceive boundaries between their group and the relevant high-status out-group as impermeable but to also see the status relations between them as illegitimate. That is, not only is it impossible to join the high-status out-group, but there is the belief that their in-group's low status is unfair. According to social identity theory, it is the combination of impermeable group boundaries and illegitimacy that allows for *cognitive alternatives* to evolve or the ability to imagine a world where one's low-status group is equal to, or even higher in status than the current high-status group of comparison. When this happens, groups will engage in *social change strategies* by banning together and fighting to improve their position.

To illustrate how this works, let's look at the #MeToo movement. To start, boundaries between the low-status group (i.e., women) and the high-status group (i.e., men) in this context are impermeable; changing groups is not possible. While women's fight for equal rights to men has been going on for over a century, the low-status position of women throughout this time has arguably wavered between perceptions of legitimacy and illegitimacy. As women have increasingly gained access to the workplace, there may have been a certain acceptance of the challenges they faced, including norms around the sexualisation and harassment that so many women have experienced by male colleagues. Indeed, as women continued to break barriers in various industries, there may not have been cognitive alternatives available to the workplace culture they were entering. However, following the allegations of sexual abuse by Hollywood producer Harvey Weinstein in 2017 and the subsequent call by celebrity Alyssa Milano for women who'd experienced harassment to use the #MeToo movement on their social media, it became apparent how widespread it was for women to experience harassment not only at work but as part of their everyday lives. With millions of women reflecting on their experiences and using the hashtag, the perception of legitimacy around women's lack of power in these settings started to change. By banding together in this common experience, women started to imagine a change to the status quo. While society is still grappling with the issue of sexual harassment, the #MeToo movement has made strides in changing how women can expect to be treated in at work.

Although I've chosen to apply social identity theory to the #MeToo movement in this instance, the theory can be used to explain any social movement or indeed any relationship between groups. It is a theory with incredible versatility in its ability to explain competition between groups, collective action and resistance, and intergroup conflict. However, it is not without its limitations. For instance, it does not tell us what conditions are necessary for perceptions of permeability and legitimacy to change (Reicher et al., 2010). Going back to our example, we might assume that the Harvey Weinstein scandal acted as a catalyst for the #MeToo movement, but this is not something the theory specifically addresses. There is also an assumption that social change can only happen when group members act collectively (rather than individually), and while this may be true based on historical evidence of social change initiatives, it is unclear exactly how a shared social identity translates into groups acting effectively to bring about this change (Reicher et al., 2010). Still, its emphasis on the role that social identity plays in contributing to our self-concept has been hugely influential. In the next section, we will turn our attention to self-categorisation theory, which aims to address some of these limitations while also addressing what happens cognitively when people categorise themselves into groups.

BOX 3.1   APPLY SOCIAL IDENTITY THEORY!

Below is a list of some recent social movements. For each, consider who the in-group and out-group are and how the behaviour of the low status might be influenced by status and by perceptions of permeability and legitimacy.

1   Extinction Rebellion
2   Black Lives Matter
3   Occupy Wallstreet
4   Women's March (2017)

SELF-CATEGORISATION THEORY

The development of self-categorisation theory (Turner et al., 1987) was led by John Turner, Henri Tajfel's PhD student and colleague. As such, the theory shares a similar ideology and makes similar assumptions as social identity theory, just with a different focus (Hornsey, 2008). To help fill in some of the gaps left by social identity theory, the aim of self-categorisation theory is to understand the cognitive aspects of the self-categorisation process and how these affect intragroup dynamics (Turner et al., 1987). According to the theory, people's self-concepts can largely be categorised along three main dimensions: the superordinate category of a human being (human identity), as a member of a social group (social identity), and by making interpersonal comparisons (personal identity). Although self-categorisation theory proposes that identity operates based on its level of inclusiveness (from being most inclusive at the human level to being least inclusive at the personal level; see Hornsey, 2008), it is like social identity theory in its premise that we mostly categorise ourselves in line with our social identities. As we discussed in Chapter 2, Turner (1982) argued that all levels of the self is a social relationship; even categorising oneself at a personal level requires interpersonal comparisons where both parties represent their respective social identities.

The aim of self-categorisation theory then is to understand how and why one identity (or category) becomes the basis for categorisation over another. In other words, of the many identities that make up our self, when does one become the basis for which we differentiate from others and how does this serve to impact who we are? Self-categorisation theory suggests that an important mechanism for determining which category will become salient is that of *fit*. Fit proposes that differences between groups are not stable, but change depending on the social dynamics that are at play at any given point (Oakes et al., 1994). With this instability in mind, fit can take two forms: *comparative fit* and *normative fit*. The former proposes that categorisation is dependent on the similarities and differences between groups, while the latter suggests that it is driven by our expectations of people based on their group membership. Reicher et al. (2010) offer a clear example of both types of fit: If psychologists and historians were in a room together, they would likely categorise themselves based on their respective disciplines. But if university business leaders walked in, then their basis for categorisation might change because now psychologists and historians have more in common with each other than they do with this new group. Exemplifying the concept of comparative fit, they might re-categorise themselves as academics and the business leaders as management. Distinction between these groups might be further enhanced (and demonstrate normative fit) if group members confirm any of the stereotypes associated with their group. For instance, if the business leaders wore suits and the academics dressed casually, then this could further cement categorisation along these group lines (see Reicher et al., 2010).

Self-categorisation theory explains that for categorisation into different groups to be possible, we go through a process called *depersonalisation*. This occurs when our view of who we are is formed based on the various characteristics associated with the group membership that has become salient. One way to think about this is that we go from 'I' to 'we' in terms of our self-concept. As part of this shift, we engage in *self-stereotyping*: defining who we are in line with how we see a particular social identity and essentially becoming representatives of that group, at least in a psychological sense (Haslam et al., 2020). This process explains how people can act so differently depending on the group identity that is salient within a given context. For instance, a man may be patient and calm when teaching his child to ride a bike, but noisy and rude when watching a football game with friends. According to self-categorisation theory, this happens because the man has categorised himself along the basis of the salient social identity (i.e., a father and a football fan) within each given context (i.e., when spending time with his child and when watching a game) and then conformed to the behaviours he associates with each (see Haslam et al., 2020).

Despite how the term itself sounds, depersonalisation is not about losing who we are. Rather, it's about how our self is continually redefined based on our categorisation with the salient social group. The man in the previous example is still a unique individual, but he has taken on the characteristics he associates with his social identities as a father and as a football fan within each context, respectively. The depersonalisation process means that when we categorise ourselves in line with a specific identity, our individual self becomes synonymous with our group self. As such, determinates of our self-esteem now involve the standing of the group, our self-interest becomes tied up with what the group values, and our self-efficacy is based on whether we think our group can achieve its aims (Haslam et al., 2020). Imagine a highly devoted fan of a particular football team. When that identity is salient (e.g., their favourite team is playing), the fan might become so subsumed by the team's performance that it is hard to believe that the fan is not part of the team itself! Indeed, whether the team wins or loses may determine the fan's mood, or even how they feel about their entire week. In this example, it is not that the fan is no longer a thinking, feeling, and acting individual; it's just that for the time being they have taken on the thoughts and feelings of their group.

In addition to its impact on our self-concept, self-stereotyping extends to our perceptions of other members of our group; not only do we see ourselves as embodying the salient group's norms, attitudes, and behaviours, but we assume that others in our group take on these traits as well. Thus, when self-stereotyping along the basis of a social category, we see both ourselves *and* our fellow in-group members as exemplifying the prototypical group member (Hornsey, 2008). This has several consequences for who we are. First, because we are emulating our understanding of the group prototype, our individual actions, feelings, and beliefs tend to align with this perception. Second, our belief that other members of our group also act in line with the group prototype colours our expectation of how they will act, feel, and what they believe. Because we share the same social identity with these others, we generally expect to agree with them on issues relevant to that domain (Haslam et al., 2020). For example, someone who identifies as a Christian will expect to agree with other Christians on issues related to religious belief and morality (although not necessarily on issues outside of the relevant domain, such as favourite sports team). They may also expect to disagree with other religions on these same domains, unless, of course, they recategorise themselves with these groups along another superordinate identity (say, as 'people of God'). Turner (1982) described this tendency to seek out what the group thinks and feels, and to respond in line with this as *referent informational influence*.

One reason that categorisation plays such a vital role in determining who we are is social influence. As discussed in Chapter 2, we depend on one another to help us navigation our social world. What self-categorisation theory proposes is that the guidance we take on and the effectiveness of that guidance on our thoughts, feelings, and behaviours depend on who we perceive to be members of our in-group members and who we see as out-group members. In this way, we engage in *social reality testing* where we look to others to determine the nature of our world and how we should act within it (Reicher et al., 2010). Take, for instance, a controversial political issue (e.g., immigration policy). When determining our opinions on this topic, we tend to look to others to shape our thinking. How those others influence us depends on their group membership with respect to our own. If I identify with the political left, I am more likely to be guided by their party's stance on the subject. At the same time, I am motivated to disagree with whatever the stance is on the political right, simply because they are the group that I do not identify with (and are seen as the out-group in this context). In this way, our group membership both guides and reinforces our individual beliefs (Reicher et al., 2010).

As with any theory, self-categorisation theory has its limitations. For instance, it has been criticised as being too simplistic, both in terms of its inability to account for the multitude of identities that we all embody and its focus on cognition at the expense of other potential motivations for categorisation. Others have questioned whether its emphasis on depersonalisation accurately captures the diversity and conflict that exists within groups (Hornsey, 2008). Regardless of these, most psychologists agree that, as with social identity theory, self-categorisation theory has revolutionised our understanding of group processes and added clarity to the link between the groups we belong to and who we are as individuals.

BOX 3.2   REAL-WORLD APPLICATION – IDENTITY AND THE PLIGHT OF REFUGEES

Five years into Syria's civil war, over 400,000 people had died and nearly 12 million people displaced from their homes. Yet, the world had largely turned a blind eye to the crisis (Slovic et al., 2017). That all changed when a photo was taken of three-year-old Aylan Kurdi, whose body had washed ashore on a beach in Turkey. He and his family had been fleeing the war-torn country when their rubber boat capsized, killing Kurdi.

The photo has been attributed to, at least temporarily, awakening people to the humanitarian crisis in Syria. In the week following the photo, daily donations to a Swedish Red Cross fund aimed specifically to help Syrian refugees increased 100-fold from the week before (Slovic et al., 2017). The photo also served as a catalyst for Western countries to soften their refugee policies, criticism of the dehumanising language being used by the media to describe people fleeing war, and an increase in people volunteering to help (Devichand, 2016).

From a social identity perspective, the image served to transform people's identification with refugees. For many, the crisis in Syria seemed far removed. As a national of a Western country, the desperation of refugees to relocate might have seemed to some as a burden on in-group resources. What the photo did was to encourage people to re-categorise themselves along a more human level of identity. Everything about the photo, from how Aylan was lying to the shoes he was wearing allowed us to connect him with our own children, and suddenly, he didn't seem so dissimilar to us. The photo's ability to transform people's thoughts, attitudes, and behaviours illustrates the power of re-categorisation.

So far in this chapter, we have covered two of the most influential theories of identity: social identity theory (Tajfel & Turner, 1979) and self-categorisation theory (Turner et al., 1987). While these two ideas may have separate focuses, their principles complement one another. Social identity theory explores social identity as an important factor in determining intergroup relations, while self-categorisation theory focuses on the cognitive aspects that make the categorisation of social identities possible (Reicher et al., 2010). Indeed, the development of self-categorisation aimed to build on and expand on some of social identity theory's fundamental principles. As such, scholars tend to refer to them under the general umbrella of the 'social identity perspective' (Hornsey, 2008). This book will follow suit; in the chapters that follow, any discussion and application of social identity on the self will encompass both theories as one general perspective. However, before we move on to these chapters, we will discuss another key identity theory called *intersectionality*. While this theory takes a different approach than what we've discussed so far, it is no less important when considering the link between identity and our self.

INTERSECTIONALITY

So far, we have been talking about social identities as if they are separate entities. Yet, this does not give a full picture of how our identities affect our self-concept. Instead, who we are consists of the way our many social identities interact and compound each other: An Asian woman does not experience the world as *just* a person of colour or as *just* a woman but lives her life with these identities simultaneously (i.e., as an Asian woman). As a result, she may face disadvantage that is not simply a result of her ethnicity or her gender, but that is specific to the interaction between these identities. A useful analogy to consider is that of a cake. It would be flawed to consider a chocolate raspberry cake as only chocolate or as only raspberry. Rather, everything about the cake (e.g., taste, appearance, etc.) depends on both ingredients (Bowleg, 2013). Intersectionality takes a similar approach to the human experience: It's a framework for understanding how people's individual experiences in the social world are impacted by the structural inequalities (e.g., racism, sexism, ableism, etc.) they experience because of their social identities (e.g., race, gender, ability; Crenshaw, 1989).

The term 'intersectionality' was coined by Kimberlé Crenshaw (1989). Crenshaw is a lawyer and an academic, who is credited with revolutionising feminism to include the challenges and experiences that are specific to women of colour. Traditionally, narratives around feminism focused on inequalities of women (versus men), while narratives around race focused on the inequalities of Black people (versus White people). This ignored people who experience inequality because of being both a woman and Black (Bowleg, 2013). Crenshaw (1989) pointed to a legal case in the United States in 1976 which exemplified this point. *In DeGraffenreid vs. General Motors (GM)*, five African American women claimed that *GM* had discriminated against them in a policy where employee redundancies were based on the length of service in the organisation. Prior to 1964, the company had never hired a Black woman (although they had hired Black men and White women). This meant that, when the 1970s recession hit, all the Black women who worked at General Motors were made redundant, as they had been at the company for the least amount of time. The plaintiffs felt that the policy disproportionately discriminated against them because of the combination of their race *and* their gender. However, because *GM* had hired both people of colour and women over the years, the complaint could not be upheld by existing laws protecting employees from gender discrimination or racial discrimination. The court simply did not have a framework to understand how people might be uniquely discriminated because of how their identities intersect.

In the over 30 years since Crenshaw's (1989) paper, research on intersectionality has recognised the interactions between other identities besides race and gender, including sexuality, class, body type, religion, nationality, and citizenship (Hankivsky, 2014). Her ideas have helped set the foundation for critical race theory, which considers how structural racism within social systems (e.g., the justice system and education) has served to reproduce the disadvantages faced by people of colour, even in the absence of individual intent for such consequences (Mohdin, 2020). In many ways, the contribution of intersectionality lies in its ability to capture the richness and complexity of social identities and the consequences these have for the way humans experience the world. McCormick-Huhn et al. (2019) highlight four ways in which intersectionality encourages us to think about people's identities. The first is that humans are multidimensional; no social group exists in isolation. By considering groups based on only one identity, we are ignoring how the other identities that people have shape our understanding of their social group. For instance, while it is true that in many contexts men are privileged compared to women, the age, race, religion, and the class of a man add additional layers of privilege and oppression to his experiences (e.g., the race of a Latinx man makes him more vulnerable to barriers in society than the race of a White man). This brings us to the second point. It is key to remember that group dynamics shift across different contexts (McCormick-Huhn et al., 2019). Hence, while men (compared to women) may be considered the high-status group within the corporate work setting, they may become the low-status group when working in female-dominated positions, such as childcare or nursing. In this way, power dynamics between groups depend on the multiple identities that make up a person and social context in which interactions take place.

Finally, intersectionality is clear about the importance of the link between people's social identities and the structural inequalities they face. Because of this, McCormick-Huhn et al. (2019) urge us not just to consider individual interventions and solutions but to broaden our thinking to include the way that existing power structures serve to perpetuate both the advantage and the disadvantage people face. It is also important to note that all of us, whether we experience advantage or disadvantage because of our identities (or likely some combination thereof), have intersectional identities and that our experience with these is linked directly to the power structures that we may or may not benefit from. We should also be careful to avoid drawing general conclusions about the privilege and oppression experienced by groups without also considering how their identities might intersect. In the example used by McCormick-Huhn et al. (2019), the conclusion that tall men are privileged compared to short men ignores the fact that Black men who are tall may be perceived as more threatening and receive more negative attention from the police compared to their shorter counterparts (Hester & Gray, 2018). Hence, intersectionality serves to broaden our thinking around how social identities impact our experiences and, by extension, who we are.

Despite recently gaining popularity, the concept of intersectionality is not new. Sojourner Truth, an American abolitionist who was born into slavery in 1797, is often attributed to exemplifying the principles of intersectionality during her 1851 speech, 'Ain't I a Woman?' (Smiet, 2021). One reason that Truth's words have continued to endure is that her illustration of the complexities involved in experiencing intersecting identities, and, importantly, having the associated challenges ignored through unidimensional approaches to understanding these, rings true for people today.

BOX 3.3 'AIN'T I A WOMAN?' SPEECH

That man over there says women need to be helped into carriages, and lifted over ditches, and have the best place everywhere. Nobody ever helps me into carriages, or over mud-puddles, or gives me any best place! And ain't I a woman? Look at me! Look at my arm! I have ploughed and planted, and gathered into barns, and no man could head me! And ain't I a woman? – Sojourner Truth (1851 Women's Convention)

CONCLUSION

Both the social identity perspective and intersectionality have made vital contributions to the way we understand identity and its impact on who we are. The former explains the role that our social identities play in shaping our perspectives of our social world, from how we categorise ourselves and others to the conditions that are necessary for social change. This perspective is one of the most influential ideas in the field of psychology. As of October 2022, Tajfel and Turner's (1979) chapter introducing the world to social identity theory had been cited over 30,726 times according to Google Scholar. The importance of intersectionality, on the other hand, lies in the framework it gives to understand the complexities of our many identities and how these are inextricably linked to existing power structures. While intersectionality was originally borne from Feminist ideology, the framework it offers has added a richness of perspective to many disciplines, both theoretical and applied (e.g., healthcare, climate change behaviours, politics; Hankivsky, 2014) and revolutionised how scholars think about people's experiences.

We started this chapter by talking about Henri Tajfel, with the aim of better understanding the path that brought him to his revolutionary ideas. As such, it seems only fitting that we end the chapter with the most recent revelations regarding Tajfel's legacy. A recent expose by Young and Hegarty (2019) described Tajfel's conduct as a professor at the University of Bristol in a way that could be, at best, described as inappropriate. Tajfel was not interested in applying his theory to women and generally had difficulty treating them as intellectual equals (Eiser, 1999). Several accounts by his former students describe numerous instances of unwanted sexual attention and bullying (Young & Hegarty, 2019). In light of these revelations, the European Association of Social Psychology, which Tajfel co-founded, announced in 2019 that they planned to rename their prestigious lifetime achievement award that bore his name. While the association stands by Tajfel's 'theoretical contribution to social psychology,' they argue that his 'reprehensible and unacceptable behaviours towards female members of his lab' make him unworthy of being characterised in a way that suggests he is a role model (EASP, 2019).

In some ways, the tarnished image of Henri Tajfel in recent years exemplifies the theories discussed in this chapter. His social identities – as a man, a professor, an immigrant – all played important roles in determining his actions, beliefs, and behaviours. Henri Tafjel, the professor, contributed a wealth of knowledge to his field, while Henri Tajfel, the man, created an environment rife with sexual harassment for his female students. Both his contribution to psychology and his behaviour around women were made possible because of existing power structures that allowed him to be both (a well-resourced professor and a man leading a department known for its 'old boys club' culture; Young & Hegarty, 2019). In fact, Young and Hegarty (2019) point out that in some ways, his position as an out-group member within his own department (he was an older immigrant among young British students and colleagues) gave his colleagues a reason to excuse him for this behaviour. If nothing else, the story of Henri Tajfel serves as an example of the complexities involved in the way that our many identities inform our self and as a reminder that unequal power structures can exist anywhere, even within the same groups devoted to studying them.

Of course, social identity theory, and our understanding of the link between one's identity and their self, has developed significantly in the years since Tajfel's death. In fact, several of his students played vital roles in extending social identity theory towards a more feminist perspective and in highlighting gender identity as integral to our concept of self (Young & Hegarty, 2019). Over the remaining four chapters, we will be drawing on recent work that uses the theories discussed here to explain how our social identities shape our understanding of the world around us and the impact that our social world has on our self-concept. We will start by discussing the role of identity in group-based behaviour, focusing specifically on social influence (Chapter 4) and intergroup relationships (Chapter 5). We will then move on to the role that language plays in shaping our identities and self-concept (Chapter 6), before moving applying these theories to real-world situations (e.g., Leadership in organisations; Chapter 7).

CHAPTER SUMMARY

- The minimal group studies revealed that just belonging to a group, even meaningless groups, will result in in-group favouritism.
- Social identity theory proposes that when an identity becomes salient, we compare it to other relevant groups. We then seek to view this identity positively by differentiating that group from others in positive ways.

- Perceptions of permeability and legitimacy determine how members of low-status groups positively distinguish themselves from high-status groups.
- Self-categorisation theory proposes that when people categorise themselves as part of a group, they take on the thoughts, feelings, and behaviours they associate with that group.
- Intersectionality considers how people's individual experiences in the social world are affected by the structural inequalities they face because of their multiple social identities.

WANT TO KNOW MORE?

Recommended Reading:
- Brown, R. (2019). *Henri Tajfel: Explorer of identity and difference*. Routledge
- Collins, P. H. (2019). *Intersectionality as critical social theory*. Duke University Press

REFERENCES

Billig, M., & Tajfel, H. (1973). Social categorization and similarity in intergroup behaviour. *European Journal of Social Psychology, 3*(1), 27–52. https://doi.org/10.1002/ejsp.2420030103

Brown, R. (2019). *Henri Tajfel: Explorer of identity and difference*. Routledge

Bowleg, L. (2013). "Once you've blended the cake, you can't take the parts back to the main ingredients": Black gay and bisexual men's descriptions and experiences of intersectionality. *Sex Roles, 68*(11), 754–767. http://10.1007/s11199-012-0152

Crenshaw, K. (1989). Demarginalizing the intersection of race and sex: A black feminist critique of antidiscrimination doctrine, feminist theory and antiracist politics. *University of Chicago Legal Forum (PhilPapers), 140*, 139–167

Devichand, M. (2016, September 2). Did Alan Kurdi's death change anything? *BBC News*. https://www.bbc.co.uk/news/blogs-trending-37257869

Doise, W., Csepeli, G., Dann, H. D., Gouge, C., Larsen, K., & Ostell, A. (1972). An experimental investigation into the formation of intergroup representations. *European Journal of Social Psychology, 2*(2), 202–204

EASP. (2019, August 1). *Renaming the Tajfel Award*. EASP Website https://www.easp.eu/news/itm/renaming_the_tajfel_award-947.html

Eiser, J. R. (1999). Interview by Sandra Cameron [Audio recording]. PSY/ TAJ/8/1: Box 64, Henry Tajfel papers, Wellcome Library, London.

Hankivsky, O. (2014). Intersectionality 101. *The Institute for Intersectionality Research & Policy, SFU,* 1–34

Haslam, S. A., Reicher, S. D., & Platow, M. J. (2020). *The new psychology of leadership: Identity, influence and power.* Routledge

Hester, N., & Gray, K. (2018). For Black men, being tall increases threat stereotyping and police stops. *Proceedings of the National Academy of Sciences, 115,* 2711–2715. http://doi.org/10.1073/pnas.1714454115

Hornsey, M. J. (2008). Social identity theory and self-categorization theory: A historical review. *Social and Personality Psychology Compass, 2*(1), 204–222. https://doi.org/10.1111/j.1751-9004.2007.00066.x

Hornsey, M. J., Spears, R., Cremers, I., & Hogg, M. A. (2003). Relations between high and low power groups: The importance of legitimacy. *Personality and Social Psychology Bulletin, 29*(2), 216–227. https://doi. org/10.1177/0146167202239047

McCormick-Huhn, K., Warner, L. R., Settles, I. H., & Shields, S. A. (2019). What if psychology took intersectionality seriously? Changing how psychologists think about participants. *Psychology of Women Quarterly, 43*(4), 445–456. https://doi.org/10.1177/0361684319866430

Mohdin, A. (2020, November 12). Kimberlé Crenshaw: The women who revolutionised feminism – and landed at the heart of the culture wars. *The Guardian.* https://www.theguardian.com/society/2020/nov/12/kimberle-crenshaw-the-woman-who-revolutionised-feminism-and-landed-at-the-heart-of-the-culture-wars

Oakes, P. J., Haslam, S. A., & Turner, J. C. (1994). *Stereotyping and social reality.* Blackwell Publishing

Platow, M. J., & Hunter, J. A. (2017). Intergroup relations and conflict: Revisiting Sherif's boys' camp studies. In J. R. Smith & S. A. Haslam (Eds.), *Social psychology: Revisiting the classic studies* (2nd Ed., pp. 146–164). Sage

Reicher, S., Spears, R., & Haslam, S. A. (2010). The social identity approach in social psychology. In M. S. Wetherell & C. T. Mohanty (Eds.), *Sage identities handbook* (pp. 45–62). Sage. http://doi.org/10.4135/9781446200889.n4

Richter, N., Over, H., & Dunham, Y. (2016). The effects of minimal group membership on young preschoolers' social preferences, estimates of similarity, and behavioral attribution. *Collabra, 2*(1). https://doi.org/10.1525/collabra.44

Slovic, P., Västfjäll, D., Erlandsson, A., & Gregory, R. (2017). Iconic photographs and the ebb and flow of empathic response to humanitarian disasters. *Proceedings of the National Academy of Sciences, 114*(4), 640–644. https://doi. org/10.1073/pnas.1613977114

Smiet, K. (2021). *Sojourner truth and intersectionality: Traveling truths in feminist scholarship.* Routledge

Tajfel, H. (1972). Experiments in a vacuum. In J. Israel & H. Tajfel (Eds.), *The context of social psychology: A critical assessment* (pp. 69–119). Academic Press

Tajfel, H., & Turner, J. C. (1979). An integrative theory of intergroup conflict. In W. G. Austin & S. Worchel (Eds.), *The social psychology of intergroup relations* (pp. 33–48). Brooks/Cole

Tajfel, H., Billig, M. G., Bundy, R. P., & Flament, C. (1971). Social categorization and intergroup behaviour. *European Journal of Social Psychology, 1*(2), 149–178. https://doi.org/10.1002/ejsp.2420010202

Turner, J. C. (1982). Towards a redefinition of the social group. In H. Tajfel (Ed.), *Social identity and intergroup relations* (pp. 15–40). Cambridge University Press

Turner, J. C., Hogg, M. A., Oakes, P. J., Reicher, S. D., & Wetherell, M. S. (1987). *Rediscovering the social group: A self-categorization theory.* Blackwell

Young, J. L., & Hegarty, P. (2019). Reasonable men: Sexual harassment and norms of conduct in social psychology. *Feminism & Psychology, 29*(4), 453–474. https://doi.org/10.1177/0959353519855746

THE SELF AS A GROUP MEMBER

Imagine you and a few friends are planning an evening out. For a long time, you've been excited to see a certain movie (let's call it *Movie X*). But when chatting to your friends, you realise that they are all keen to see a different movie (*Movie Y*). As the conversation goes on, you realise that no one seems at all interested in *Movie X* and, in fact, some of them have mentioned hearing negative reviews of it. A friend turns to you to ask for your opinion. Without thinking you find yourself expressing enthusiasm for *Movie Y*, failing to even mention *Movie X* as an option.

Most of us can relate to this situation in one way or another. But why does this happen? We've already discussed the importance of others in shaping our thoughts, feelings, and behaviours. Here, we will discuss some of the more extreme examples of how others can influence us. For instance, can you imagine claiming that the sky is green because the strangers around you have? Or that you would be more likely to help someone in need based on a characteristic as arbitrary as their clothing? And, most seriously, that you might kill another human being because someone told you to?

Most of us would like to think that we would always do the right thing – that we would remain truthful to what we know to be real, that we would be happy to help anyone that needed us, and that we would never knowingly harm (much less kill) another person. And yet, much of the research in psychology tells us that whatever we'd like to think about what we would do, how we behave in these circumstances largely depends on our relationship with those around us. In this chapter, we will focus on how group dynamics shape our

DOI: 10.4324/9780429274534-4

behaviour. Taking a social identity perspective, we will discuss the role of what is arguably the most important influence on our behaviour in a social situation: who we identify with and who we do not.

EARLY WORK ON SOCIAL INFLUENCE

Psychologists use the term 'social influence' to describe when individuals change their beliefs and behaviours to meet the real or perceived demands of others. Although we may be aware of the effect others have on us, influence often happens without us realising it. For example, while in a shop, most of us wouldn't dream of pushing people out of the way so that we can pay first; instead, we join the back of the queue. We don't necessarily think about this – it's just something that we do automatically.

One of the earliest studies on social influence was conducted by Muzafar Sherif in the early 1930s. In what became a landmark study, Sherif (1935) asked participants to observe the amount of movement made by a pinpoint of light while sitting in a dark room. In a visual illusion known as the 'autokinetic effect,' a stationary light appears to move around spontaneously. He found that when individual participants were asked how much the light moved, their answers varied between 2 and 6 inches. However, when participants were asked in groups, their answers quickly converged to an average position (e.g., 4 inches).

To explain his findings, Sherif (1936) argued that the change in participant's perceptions of their experience during the study had been shaped by the norms that emerged during the group task. As explained in Chapter 2, norms refer to the implicit or explicit rules that a group has for acceptable beliefs, values, and behaviours. According to Sherif (1936), a norm had been formed by participants emphasising compromise and finding common ground. Because groups have the power to influence our thoughts and beliefs, the group-based perception of the light's movement superseded participant's individual one.

In addition to shaping immediate perceptions, research has shown that adjustments that are made based on group norms affect participant's memories of the event. Using a similar paradigm, Rohrer and colleagues (1954) moved the light either two inches or

8 inches before asking for participants' estimates as individuals. Following this, they assigned participants to groups (one participant from each session) and exposed them to the stationary light (the autokinetic effect). Like with Sherif's (1935) study, participants also converged their estimates: the 2-inch participants converged from 3.08 inches to 6.29 inches, while the 8-inch participants converged from 8.74 inches to 6.41 inches). A year later, the researchers tested the same participants individually using the stationary light. Despite the amount of time that had passed, participants' answers more closely resembled the earlier group position than their own initial individual one (5.50 inches and 5.09 inches, respectively). Hence, despite the absence of that group norm for a year, its influence still held.

Research by Soloman Asch further demonstrates the power others have to influence our perceptions. In one of his early investigations into the topic of social influence, Asch (1948) conducted a study where American participants were told that the following sentence had been said either by Thomas Jefferson (America's third president) or by Vladimir Lenin (the first leader of Soviet Russia): "I hold it that a little rebellion, now and again, is a good thing, and as necessary in the political world as storms are in the physical." When participants believed the statement was made by Jefferson, they tended to agree with it, equating the word 'rebellion' with minor agitation. However, when participants thought the speaker was Lenin, they mostly disagreed with it, believing that the word 'rebellion' in this context meant 'violent revolution' (Asch, 1948). In short, this study showed that participants' attitude towards and interpretation of the message depended on their perceptions of the speaker. We will go in more depth about the link between language and influence in Chapter 6.

This early evidence demonstrates the power others have to shape our self. In the following sections, we will explore this influence within the following areas: conformity, obedience, tyranny, and helping. After reviewing some of psychology's seminal research on these topics, we will look at these studies through the perspective of social identity. Specifically, we will explore how the participant's relationships with other people in these experiments affected how they chose to act.

CONFORMITY

While the research on social influence provided psychologists with
initial understandings about the influence of others, Asch noted that
their designs (i.e., judging the movement of light, giving opinions
on a quote) meant that the consequences for changing one's beliefs
were minimal. To understand the effects of social influence more
thoroughly, Asch set out to test whether people's fundamental
beliefs could be changed because of those around them.

The result of this effort was his famous conformity studies (Asch,
1955). In these studies, male university students were asked to participate in a 'psychological study of visual judgement.' The students
were seated around a table facing an experimenter. The experiment
would put a card on the board that contained one standard line
followed by three comparison lines. One of the comparison lines
was identical to the standard line (Line 1), while the other two were
noticeably shorter. Each participant was asked in turn to match the
standard line with the most similar comparison line. This process
was repeated across 12 trials.

In the first two trials, the participants' answers are obviously correct (i.e., they say 'one'). But in Trial 3 the participants answer
incorrectly (i.e., they say 'two'). This happens again in Trials 4, 6,
7, 9, and 12. What was going on? It turns out that only one of the
participants in the study was an actual participant; the rest were
actors (or as we say in psychology, 'confederates') who had been
trained by the experimenter to give the incorrect answer. Asch had
designed this study to investigate how people would respond when
put in a situation where there was social pressure from others to
question what they knew to be true (in this case, the length of
lines).

The results show that 76% of (actual) participants went along
with the confederate's incorrect answer at least once over the 12
trials (Asch, 1952). It turns out that participants' decision to conform to something they knew to be untrue was shaped by their
perceptions of the others in the situation. Asch (1955) noted that
many participants saw themselves, rather than the others, as the
source of the problem. For example, some thought they might be
experiencing a problem with their vision. The assumption made by
these participants was that if others saw it differently, then it must

be them that that was wrong. Psychologists call this logic *informational influence* or the belief that the answer given by the majority must be correct. Others assumed that it was the first 'participant' who was mistaken and that everyone else had repeated their answer to save them the embarrassment. These reasons suggest that participants were actively trying to make sense of the situation and to facilitate what they interpreted to be the group's goals.

Another reason that participants conformed was to avoid the social consequences of going against the group majority. These might include confrontation, ridicule, or even ostracism. When people conform because the fear of standing out as different outweighs the motivation to be accurate, we call it *normative influence* or conforming to be accepted. Research supports the premise that the fear of going against the group helps explain participants' choice to conform. In a follow-up study, Asch reversed his paradigm by placing one confederate among 16 participants. When the confederate gave the wrong answer, he was mocked for it (Asch, 1955). In another study, Deutch and Gerard (1955) eliminated the fear of ridicule by allowing participants to write their answers down privately. In this version of the paradigm, conformity dropped to 12.5%.

It is important to note, however, that not everyone conformed; 24% of participants never conformed and only 11% conformed on all of the trials. In fact, each time the participant said the wrong answer in line with the group majority, he resisted the group's influence by saying the right answer twice. Although there is still work to be done to understand why people resist conforming, the message from Asch's work is that participants navigate situations based on how they perceive those around them (Jetten & Hornsey, 2017). His studies demonstrate that human beings rely on other human beings to make sense of a situation, especially when those situations are ambiguous (see Chapter 2). Even when we know intellectually what is correct, how others behave can call our thinking into question, and even encourage us to doubt ourselves.

While Asch's conformity studies were instrumental in demonstrating the importance of others in shaping how we view the world, what is 'correct' is not always as straightforward as whether one line is the same size as another. With this in mind, we turn our attention to what are perhaps the most famous experiments in all of psychology: Milgram's 'obedience' studies.

OBEDIENCE

Like many social psychologists of his time, Stanley Milgram's research interests were shaped by the horrors of the Holocaust: what led the Nazis to persecute over 6 million people, mainly Jews? And why did seemingly normal people go along with a plan that surely ran counter to their values? To investigate this, he set out to design an experiment that would capture the darkest side of human behaviour. The result of this effort is his 'obedience to authority' studies, which remain some of the most notorious and influential studies of all time.

Milgram advertised for male subjects to take part in a study on 'memory and learning.' When participants arrived at the lab, they always did so at the same time as another person. An experimenter then randomly assigned the participant to the role of 'Teacher' and the other person to the role of 'Learner,' and placed them in separated rooms, connected through an intercom. The Teacher was sat in front of a shock machine and told by the 'Experimenter' to give an electric shock to the 'Learner' every time he made an error on a word-recall task. The shocks increased by 15 volts over 30 increments (from 15 volts – a 'slight shock' – to 140 volts, labelled as XXX; Milgram, 1974).

What the participant did not know was that the shocks were fake, and the Learner was not another participant but a confederate of Milgram's. The experiment was also not actually about memory and learning. Rather, Milgram was interested in how far the participants would go (i.e., how many electric volts they would administer) at the request of the 'Experimenter.' The experiment was carefully constructed so that the 'Learner' followed a similar script for each participant: at 90 volts he screamed out in pain, at 150 volts he complained that his heart was bothering him and insisted he wanted to stop the study, and at 345 volts he stopped responding all together. The 'Experimenter' also followed a script by adhering to four prods in sequence: if the 'Teacher' (i.e., the real participant) hesitated, the 'Experimenter' would say 'Please continue' (Prod 1). If the 'Teacher' continued to hesitate, he would say 'The experiment requires that you continue' (Prod 2) followed by 'It is absolutely essential that you continue' (Prod 3). If after being given all three prods, the 'Teacher' still hesitated, the 'Experimenter' would move to Prod 4: 'You have no other choice, you must go on.' In a result that was said to 'shock the world' (e.g., Blass, 2004) Milgram (1963) reported that in his 'baseline study' every participant administered at least 300 volts (labelled on the shock machine as 'intense shocks'). Furthermore, 65% of them reached the end of the study, administering volts of electricity that would have proved lethal to the 'Learner.'

But what exactly do these results mean? From research that has investigated Milgram's archives, we know that he considered several explanations for his findings (Haslam et al., 2015). However, in this 1974 book, he settled on one, which he called the 'agentic state model of obedience.' Here, Milgram argued that when in the presence of an authority figure, people are predisposed to do what they are told. According to this account, people become so focused on following the orders of the person in charge, they lose sight of the consequences of their actions (Milgram, 1974). In other words, people blindly follow the orders of authority, even if that means behaving in a way that they might otherwise consider to be abhorrent.

At this point, it is worth noting that Milgram would have formulated this 'agentic state' explanation around the same time that political theorist Hannah Arendt attended the 1961 trial of Adolf Eichmann, the chief organiser of the Holocaust. In her book that followed, she famously coined the phrase 'the banality of evil' after observing that Eichmann did not look like the monster that everyone expected to see entering the courtroom, but rather like an everyday bureaucrat (Arendt, 1963). His claim that he was simply doing his job seemed to support the idea that anyone (even seemingly ordinary people) could become embroiled in horrific behaviours. Like Milgram's 'agentic state' model of obedience, she argued that, when in the presence of their superiors, ordinary people are capable of extraordinary evil because they will follow what they are told to do (Haslam & Reicher, 2007). The narrative that people are prone to 'follow orders' that was brought together by both Milgram and Arendt has been enormously influential across a range of fields and has been used to explain people's behaviour in a variety of contexts. Part of its appeal may well be its ability to offer a simple yet compelling explanation for some of the most horrific acts committed by human beings.

However, psychologists have begun to question the idea that people blindly go along with others. Much of this research has been inspired by evidence suggesting that in contrast to Milgram's proposed 'agentic state,' people do not simply do as they are told. Rather, they go along with others because of their belief in the person or in the cause the person is seen to represent. In other words, obedience is contingent on identity: The more people identify with the authority figure and/or their cause, the more willing they are to go along with what they are being asked to do (Haslam & Reicher, 2012). Historians have also questioned the idea that Adolf Eichmann, the inspiration for Arendt's 'banality of evil' hypothesis, was an ordinary man simply doing as he was told. Rather, he was aware of the suffering he was causing and, while always comfortable with Nazi ideology, became increasingly dedicated to the goal of the extermination of Jews as the war progressed (Haslam & Reicher, 2007). In fact, he was so devoted to this plan that he challenged his superior, Heinrich Himmler, over plans that would have saved Jewish lives (Cesarani, 2005). Hence, the murders committed by Eichmann cannot be attributed to doing what he was told, but rather, to his goal of extinguishing an entire race of people.

To illustrate the link between identity and behaviour, imagine you have two psychology lecturers who take different approaches to engage students with weekly readings. One uses fear, by warning that you will fall behind and that your mark will suffer if you don't do the reading. The other emphasises the goals you share, by explaining how the readings benefit your learning and how they will help you to achieve higher marks. Consider the approach that is more likely to motivate you and why that might be. Now, let's say both lecturers ask for volunteers to help put chairs away after a teaching session. The social identity approach would predict that you would be more likely to help the second lecturer. This is because their approach to teaching will mean you are more likely to identify with them, making you more likely to do what they ask (even if it's with something you might not particularly want to do, like put chairs away!).

The idea that people obey (or follow along with) authority figures because they identify with them is known as the 'engaged followership model of obedience' (Haslam & Reicher, 2012). In addition to the historical accounts of the role that identity played in perpetuating the Holocaust, some of the most compelling evidence for this model lies in Milgram's own work. Although the results of the 'baseline study' are the most commonly known, Milgram ran over 30 versions of this study. In these, obedience ranged from 10% to 100% depending on variations in their design (Milgram, 1974). For example, when the study was run on a commercial estate in Bridgeport, Connecticut, rather than at the prestigious Yale University laboratories, obedience dropped to 48%. When the 'Experimenter' gave his instructions to the 'Teacher' by phone rather than in person, obedience dropped to 9%. When Milgram varied how physically close the participants were to the 'Learner', he found that the closer they were, the less obedient participants became (Milgram, 1974).

The different responses of participants across Milgram's studies cannot be explained by the 'agentic state' account. If people enter a state in which they cede all responsibility to their superiors, then obedience would have remained consistent throughout Milgram's studies. Also, the design of the 'baseline study' was such that it would have encouraged identification with the 'Experimenter' rather than with the Learner. For instance, the fact that the participant was in the same room as the 'Experimenter' (while the Learner was in a different room) would have ensured a closer bond with the former than with the latter. Milgram also made sure that the 'Experimenter' stressed the study's importance as the first research investigating the effect of punishment on learning (Milgram, 1963) and was careful to present himself as a prototypical scientist. These details would have ensured a stronger sense of obligation to the 'Experimenter' than to the 'Learner' (Reicher & Haslam, 2011).

There is also experimental evidence of the role identity plays when people obey (see Birney et al., 2022). One example involves the prods used by the 'Experimenter.' Of the four prods, the fourth (i.e., 'You have no other choice, you must go on') is the only one that resembles an order. If you look at the data from Milgram's baseline study, it is also the only one where no one chooses to continue with the study after receiving it (Burger et al., 2011). To explore this further, an experiment was conducted where participants were given one of the four prods in an online (and ethical) version of Milgram's paradigm. As expected, the researchers found that the fourth order-like prod was the least successful in encouraging participants to continue with the study (Haslam et al., 2014). Interestingly, however, the most successful prod was Prod 2 (i.e., 'The experiment requires that you continue'). In other words, when the prod reminded participants of their promise to the 'Experimenter' to complete the study, they were more likely to continue with the task.

For good reason, today's ethical standards prevent researchers from testing models of obedience using Milgram's study design. As a result, psychologists have had to rely on alternative paradigms such as virtual reality (Gonzalez-Franco et al., 2018), online studies (Birney et al., 2022), digital immersive realism (Haslam et al., 2015), correlational designs (Reicher et al., 2012), and analyses of Milgram's archives (Haslam et al, 2015b). Although none of these methods can match the drama of Milgram's paradigm, cumulatively they support an 'engaged followership' explanation of obedience rather than the 'agentic state' account. The implications of this are great. In short, we should not excuse behaviour on the grounds that the perpetrator was 'just following orders' or because going along with an authority figure is an innate tendency that we all have. Rather, based on evidence that people's willingness to obey authority is due to their belief in the ideas or goals that the authority figure represents, those who commit atrocities against others should be held responsible for their actions.

TYRANNY

Just as identity plays a role when individuals follow others' requests to engage in abhorrent behaviour, so too should identity be considered when power is abused by groups. With this in mind, we turn our attention to tyranny. Tyranny can be characterised by cruel, harsh, and unfair treatment by people with power in a society. The shocking abuses of Iraqi prisoners by American soldiers at Abu Ghraib prison in 2004 is just one example of the extreme brutality that has been imposed on non-powerful groups by groups with power. That particular case continues to capture the imagination of the public with many asking the same question that social psychologist, Philip Zimbardo, asked in 2007: How is it possible that "the fine young men and women sent overseas on the glorious mission of bringing democracy and freedom to Iraq could contemplate, let alone perpetuate, such acts?" (Zimbardo, 2007: 324).

It was this question that Zimbardo himself sought to answer with his now infamous Stanford Prison Experiment (SPE). In 1971, Zimbardo recruited 24 male university students to participate in a study that would take place in a simulated prison. According to the pre-selection interviews, participants were emotionally stable, intelligent, and mature. None of them showed signs of having a particularly authoritarian personality (Zimbardo, 1971). Participants were randomly assigned to the role of 'Guard' or 'Prisoner': Participants in the Guard role wore khaki shirts and trousers, had a whistle and a nightstick, and wore reflective glasses. They were also allowed to go home after their eight-hour shifts. Participants in the Prisoner role wore chains on one ankle, smocks with no underwear, rubber sandals, and a cap made from nylon. Unlike the Guards, they were not allowed to go home, staying in the prison for the duration of the study (Zimbardo, 2004).

Zimbardo reported that the relationship between the Guards and the Prisoners became so toxic that the study had to be cut short after only 6 days. Although the beginning of the study saw participants feeling uncertain as to how to behave, the dynamic changed when one of the Guards (nicknamed 'John Wayne') seemed to enjoy exercising his power. He started calling Prisoners by their numbers rather than their names, forcing them to do press-ups, and putting them in solitary confinement for minor infractions. Angry and frustrated, the Prisoners started engaging in acts of rebellion (e.g., swearing at the Guards, barricading themselves in their cells, etc.). Before long, tyranny ensued. The Guards started breaking into cells, stripping Prisoners naked, and forcing them to wash toilets with their bare hands. Zimbardo then made himself the 'Prison Warden' and only ended the study after his girlfriend visited the site and expressed her dismay at the situation she found there (Zimbardo, 2004).

Importantly, Zimbardo maintains that participants received no prior training or instruction on how they should behave while in the prison (Hanley et al., 1973). Hence, to explain the tyrannical relationship that formed over the course of the study, Zimbardo reported that participants naturally fell into the roles that they were given and that the brutality that resulted was due to the toxic situation they were in. This explanation was in stark contrast to previous understandings of tyranny, which assumed that perpetrators' behaviours are related to some pathology or defunct personality trait. In an analogy used by Zimbardo to illustrate his belief in the power a situation has to transform behaviour, he claimed that people who take part in horrific abuses of power are not necessarily 'bad apples' but rather find themselves in a 'bad barrel' (Zimbardo, 2004).

The SPE has been enormously influential, largely due to its focus away from explaining behaviour using a person's disposition towards one that considers people's environment. However, the study has also attracted criticism over its methodology. One such criticism centres around the Experimenters' roles as the prison's Warden and whether their presence, and their lack of intervention when abuses started, created norms for the Guards' behaviour. Another criticism involves questions over the exact level of instruction Guards were given. While Zimbardo remains adamant that participants acted on their own accord, there has been ample evidence to suggest that he encouraged the Guards' brutality (Haslam et al., 2019). Hence, without a better understanding of the role that these factors might have played in influencing participants' behaviour, it is not possible to conclude that tyranny is borne purely out of the situation people find themselves.

Inspired by the SPE, and the questions it raises about intergroup behaviour and tyranny, social psychologists Stephen Reicher and Alex Haslam recreated Zimbardo's paradigm. The study, which was conducted in conjunction with the British Broadcasting Company (BBC), is known as the *BBC Prison Study* (BPS). Like in Zimbardo's study, the researchers created a prison-like environment, randomly assigning 15 men to the role of either 'Prisoner' or 'Guard.' However, unlike in Zimbardo's study, Reicher and Haslam (2006) ensured that as the Experimenters, they had no formal role in the 'prison.' They also took a different perspective on tyranny, exploring it from a social identity perspective. Reicher and Haslam (2006) surmised that role adoption would depend on identification; participants would only take up roles (and behaviours associated with those roles) when they were identified with that group. Based on this, they expected that identification would play a key role in determining not only when people go along with oppressive groups but also when people resist and challenge the oppression they face (Haslam & Reicher, 2012).

The ending of the BPS mirrored that of SPE. After 8 days tyranny ensued, prompting the researchers to cut the study short. However, the path that led to this point was different to that which was seen in the SPE. First, without Experimenters' involvement in the running of the prison, the Guards struggled to reach a consensus among themselves on how the prison should operate. Without a shared identity, the Guards become ineffective and disorganised. Meanwhile, the Prisoners developed a strong sense of identity, which facilitated them to resist the unequal society they found themselves. As a result of this dynamic, a 'commune' was developed in which both Guards and Prisoners came together to run the prison as a collective. This arrangement began as a success, with participants working more effectively together than they did as separate groups. However, due to a few participants feeling marginalised in this structure and to some chance misunderstandings, proposals were made by four participants to introduce a new, more extreme, hierarchical system (Reicher & Haslam, 2006). Supporters of the 'commune' became despondent, reportedly because they were aware that the current system was not working and therefore felt relieved to hand responsibility over to someone else. However, the ethical guidelines being adhered to by the researchers prohibited the type of hierarchy being proposed, and so the researchers ended the study before it could be implemented.

Based on their findings in the BPS, Reicher and Haslam (2006) agree with Zimbardo that tyranny cannot be understood by focusing solely on the characteristics of individuals. Rather, the situation plays a vital role in understanding the behaviour of groups with different levels of power. However, the results of the BPS challenge the notion put forward by Zimbardo that group behaviour is somehow mindless or naturally antisocial. Instead, Reicher and Haslam (2006) argue that group values, norms, and behaviours depend on the group's shared identification and that this can be pro-social as well as anti-social. In contrast to Zimbardo's message that groups in power will automatically become tyrannical, the BPS shows that it is when groups fail (i.e., they cannot create a functioning system, people feel powerless) that they become more likely to accept (and less likely to resist) the tyrannical rule. This idea has been supported by recent work by Sprong et al. (2019) who found that the desire for a 'strong' leader to restore order (even to the point of challenging democratic values) was attractive to people in societies experiencing large social inequalities.

For a long time, the dispute over how much guidance Guards received made it impossible for psychologists to reach a consensus on the role identity played in the SPE. However, this changed in 2018 when Zimbardo's archive at Stanford University was made available to the public online. This new evidence made clear that the Experimenters in the SPE not only directed the Guards behaviour but actively encouraged them to engage in brutality (La Textier, 2018). In fact, when one of the Guards resisted acting cruelly towards the Prisoners, he was confronted by the Warden and was told he needed to 'get involved,' to act more 'tough,' and to embrace the role of the 'stereotype Guard.' In a prime example of identity leadership (see Chapter 7), the Warden tried to create a shared identity with the reluctant Guard and drew on this to encourage him. He stated that they both wanted policies that would support the rehabilitation of prisoners but reminded him that political change depended on Guards acting in a way that would shock and appal the public. Accordingly, he claimed that the study could be used to make 'recommendations for prison reform' but that this goal could be thwarted if participants assigned as Guards resisted acting cruelly towards the Prisoners (Haslam et al., 2019).

This new evidence, coupled with the results of the BPS, suggests that identity plays a key role in determining how unequal groups behave towards one another. Whether that identity emerges naturally (as in the BPS) or is created by the Experimenters (as in SPE), it helps to establish the norms and the behaviours that people are willing to follow or to reject. Much like the role of identity on willingness to obey, people do not engage in tyranny naturally or blindly, but do so based on their identification with the group and their goals.

HELPING BEHAVIOUR

On 13th March 1964, Kitty Genovese was attacked as she walked towards her home in New York City. Over a period of 30 minutes, she was stabbed repeatedly and sexually assaulted before being murdered by her attacker. Eleven days later the *New York Times* ran a front-page story about the case. In it, they claimed that 38 people had witnessed the attack but that none had intervened or phoned for help. Although we now know that this article was rife with inaccuracies (Manning et al., 2007), at the time it led to a fierce debate about whether city-living had contributed to a breakdown of moral and social values. Of the topics we've covered in this chapter, the question this debate inspired may feel the most relevant to your own life. Most of us have asked the following question: If there is an emergency and I need help, how likely am I to get it?

When reflecting on the Kitty Genovese case, and when interpreting the results from their later experiments, social psychologists Bibb Latané and John Darley made two observations about helping in emergencies. First, while it is usually clear in hindsight that an emergency has taken place, it is usually less obvious at the time. As Darley stated, "Emergencies don't come with a sign saying 'I am an emergency'" (Darley, in Evans 1980: 216). To decipher whether a situation is urgent, people tend to look to how others react. Yet, this strategy may be misleading. For instance, if others appear unconcerned about what they are seeing, then this may establish a norm of inaction and act as a deterrent from helping, even if the situation requires it. The idea that the inaction of others can result in our own inaction is known as *pluralistic ignorance* (Latané & Darley, 1968). The second point is that, even if the event is interpreted as an emergency, it does not automatically follow that a person will assume the responsibility for providing help. When multiple people are present, it may be unclear who should act. This can lead to what Latané and Darley described as a *diffusion of responsibility*, where, as the number of people present increases, the level of responsibility taken on by individuals decreases. These processes result in what is known as the *bystander effect*. This proposes that the more people present during an emergency, the less likely anyone is to step in and help.

These ideas were empirically tested by Latané and Darley in two studies that are regarded as classics in Psychology. In both studies, the aim of the researchers was to investigate whether the presence of others would deter people from providing help during a (fake) emergency. In the 'seizure' experiment, undergraduate psychology students were asked to take part in a study supposedly exploring personal problems faced by university students (Darley & Latané, 1968). Participants were placed in separate rooms and told they would be communicating with others via intercoms; each discussant would have two minutes to speak, while all other microphones were turned off. To (supposedly) ensure that everyone would feel comfortable sharing, they were also told that the experimenter would not be listening to the conversations but would be assessing individual contributions later via a questionnaire. This way, when faced with the (staged) emergency, participants would not assume that help would come from the experimenter.

Of course, the people that participants were conversing with were not actually participants but recordings. The experimenters varied whether participants thought they were alone, with one other 'participant,' or with four other 'participants.' This was to test how the presence of others would influence (1) whether the real participant would seek help and (2) how long it would take for them to do so. The 'emergency' occurred when, over the course of the discussion, one of the supposed 'participants' (i.e., the recordings) mentioned suffering from seizures before appearing to have a serious one that could be heard over the intercom. As expected, and in line with the bystander effect, participants who thought they were alone helped the most and the fastest (85% of the time taking an average of 52 seconds), followed by participants with one other bystander (62% of the time taking an average of 96 seconds), and lastly participants with four other bystanders (31% of the time taking an average of 166 seconds; Darley & Latané, 1968).

A similar pattern was found during the 'white smoke' experiment (Latané & Darley, 1968). In this study, male university students were asked to take part in a study investigating problems relevant to students at urban universities. After arriving to the lab, participants were asked to sit in a waiting room and complete a questionnaire. While filling in the survey, the experimenters organised for the room to fill up with a (harmless) white smoke. As in the 'seizure' experiment, they varied group size (participants were either alone in the waiting room or with two others) and measured whether the participant reported the smoke as well as the length of time it took them to report it. As expected, alone participants helped more than those in groups of three (75% vs. 38%, respectively) and were faster to report the smoke (after two minutes, 55% of alone participants had reported the smoke compared to 12% of those with others present). Furthermore, when the other participants were confederates trained to act indifferent to the situation, participants only reported the smoke 10% of the time (Latané & Darley, 1968; see also Levine, 2017).

Based on these studies, Latané and Darley (1970) proposed a five-step model to explain behaviour during emergencies. These consisted of the following: noticing the event (step 1), interpreting it as an emergency (step 2), assuming responsibility (step 3), evaluating potential options and deciding how to act (step 4), and finally, implementing a decision (step 5). They argued that pluralistic ignorance and the diffusion of responsibility serve to impede this process at steps 2 and 3, respectively. Today, the bystander effect remains one of the most reliable findings in psychology (Latané & Nida, 1981). However, what role does identity play in this process? From a social identity perspective, it follows that engaging in helping behaviour might be influenced by the following: the identity of the (potential) helper, whether their identity is shared with the other bystanders or with the person needing help, and the norms that are associated with that identity (see Levine, 2017). Although Latané and Darley's research suggests that others can impede helping, it is also possible that having a shared identity with those others could promote helping.

To investigate the role of identity, Levine and colleagues (2005) ran several cleverly devised experiments. In one experiment, fans of the Manchester United football team were asked to write an essay about their team, a task aimed to remind participants of that social identity. Participants were then asked to walk to another building for the next part of the study. While on route, a confederate tripped, fell, and cried out in pain in the presence of the participant. Importantly, the confederate was wearing a Manchester United shirt (in-group identity), a shirt by a rival team (out-group identity), or an unbranded shirt (control group). As expected, when the confederate shared the same identity as the participant, they received help 92% of the time (compared to 30% of the time for the out-group identity and 33% of the time for the control). These results were replicated in a second study where Manchester United fans were asked to write about their love of football generally (rather than their love of their favourite team). This task served to remind participants of their identity as a football fan (rather than just as a fan of a particular team). The results showed that the confederate who wore the rival team t-shirt received help almost as often (70%) as the confederate wearing the Manchester United shirt (80%), presumably because both identities (football fan) were now shared. The confederate who wore the unbranded shirt (i.e., who did not visibly share an identity with the participant) only received help 22% of the time (Levine et al., 2005).

But how does identity influence helping in the presence of others? Again, Levine and Crowther (2008) found that this depends on the identity of those others. In this study, which was supposedly exploring the relationship between gender and violence, participants were asked to watch CCTV footage of a man acting aggressively towards a woman on a city street. Participants were then asked via a questionnaire about their willingness to help the victim either alone or in groups of three. These groups were either all male, all female, or mixed sex. Results indicated that women reported more willingness to help when grouped with other women than when alone but were unwilling to help when in a group with two other men. Men reported similar levels of willingness when alone or with other men, but especially willing to help when in a group with two other women. This pattern was repeated when confederates staged a situation where a female graduate student was spoken to rudely by a male graduate student. Hence, it seems that although the size of the group does impact on people's helping behaviour, so too does the amount of shared social identity that people have with others in the situation – both the other bystanders and the victim.

Although the Kitty Genovese case inspired research on the bystander effect, the claim that there were 38 witnesses to the attack was wholly inaccurate. In fact, only three witnesses saw Genovese and her attacker together, and several tried to intervene by shouting and even phoning the local police station. This willingness to help a stranger is also supported by recent evidence. Drawing from CCTV footage across three different countries, Philpot et al. (2019) found that in 90% of emergencies, at least one person helped. They also found that higher numbers of bystanders made it more likely that someone would intervene. This is not to suggest that the bystander effect is untrue. Rather, this evidence suggests that the factors influencing helping may be more complex than what can possibly be captured in a lab. However, given the evidence of the role that identity plays in determining whether people offer help, it is important that it is not ignored in research going forward.

CONCLUSION

As human beings, we depend on each other for almost everything – from having someone to see a movie with to helping us meet our most basic needs for survival. As our physical and social world depends on the presence of others, it's not surprising that we are deeply influenced by those around us. Yet for a long time our understanding of social influence has centred around the idea that when people are with others, they are prone to toxic behaviour. Indeed, many of the classic studies in psychology seem to show that the presence of others results in people conforming to behaviour that they know is wrong, obeying harmful instructions, abusing their power, and failing to help those in need. However, when you view this work through the lens of identity, it becomes clear that social influence does not automatically lead to such bleak outcomes. In these same studies, there are instances of people facilitating group goals, challenging toxic authority, resisting inequality, and helping. What makes the difference in behaviour? It seems that whether we go along with others' behaviours depends largely on how much we identify with them and/or the cause they represent. Hence, it is important to remember that, just as the presence of others can tap into the worst in a person, it also has the potential to harness the best.

CHAPTER SUMMARY

- Group norms can impact both our current perceptions and our memories of an event.
- Asch's conformity studies demonstrate that even when we know something is true, others' behaviours can cause us to doubt our judgement.
- While Milgram's 'obedience to authority' studies have traditionally been understood as showing that people follow orders, more recent interpretations of their results suggest that obedience depends on people's identification with others in the social context.

- Evidence from both the SPE's archives and the BPS shows that tyranny results when people identify with group norms that encourage brutality.
- While the bystander effect – the phenomenon where the more people who witness an emergency the less likely anyone is to help – has been shown in the lab, CCTV footage of real-world emergencies shows that in most cases people are willing to help. Research also suggests that the identity that a potential helper shares with others in the social situation can serve to both encourage and inhibit their willingness to help others.

WANT TO KNOW MORE?

Recommended Reading:
- Smith, J. R., & Haslam, S. A. (2017). *Social psychology: Revisiting the classic studies.* Sage

REFERENCES

Arendt, H. (1963). *Eichmann in Jerusalem: A report on the banality of evil.* Penguin

Asch, S. E. (1948). The doctrine of suggestion, prestige, and imitation in social psychology. *Psychological Review, 55*(5), 250–276. https://doi.org/10.1037/h0057270

Asch, S. E. (1952). *Social psychology.* Prentice-Hall

Asch, S. E. (1955). Opinions and social pressure. *Scientific American, 193*(5), 31–35

Birney, M. E., Reicher, S. D., Haslam, S. A., Steffens, N. K., & Nevile, F. G. (2022), Engaged followership and toxic science: Exploring the effect of prototypicality on willingness to follow harmful experimental instructions. British Journal of Social Psychology, 00, 1–17. https://doi.org/10.1111/bjso.12603

Blass, T. (2004). The man who shocked the world: The life and legacy of Stanley Milgram. New York: Basic Books, 2004

Burger, J. M., Girgis, Z. M., & Manning, C. M. (2011). In their own words: Explaining obedience to authority through an examination of participants' comments. *Social Psychological and Personality Science, 2*, 460–466. https://doi.org/10.1177/1948550610397632

Cesarani, D. (2005). *Eichmann: His life and crimes.* Random House

Darley, J. M., & Latane, B. (1968). Bystander intervention in emergencies: Diffusion of responsibility. *Journal of Personality and Social Psychology, 8*(4, Pt.1), 377–383. https://doi.org/10.1037/h0025589

Deutsch, M., & Gerard, H. B. (1955). A study of normative and informational social influences upon individual judgment. *The Journal of Abnormal and Social Psychology, 51*(3), 629–636. https://doi.org/10.1037/h0046408

Evans, R. I. (1980). *The making of social psychology.* Gardner Press, Inc.

Gonzalez-Franco, M., Slater, M., Birney, M. E., Swapp, D., Haslam, S. A., & Reicher, S. D. (2018). Participant concerns for the learner in a virtual reality replication of the Milgram obedience study. *PLoS One, 13.* http://doi.org/10.1371/journal.pone.0209704

Hanley, C., Banks, C., & Zimbardo, P. (1973). A study of prisoners and guards in a simulated prison. *Naval Research Reviews,* September: 1–17. Washington D.C: Office of Naval Research

Haslam, S. A., & Reicher, S. (2007). Beyond the banality of evil: Three dynamics of an interactionist social psychology of tyranny. *Personality and Social Psychology Bulletin, 33*(5), 615–622. https://doi.org/10.1177/0146167206298570

Haslam, S. A., & Reicher, S. (2017). Tyranny: Revisiting Zimbardo's Stanford prison experiment. In J. R. Smith & S. A. Haslam (Eds.), *Social psychology: Revisiting the classic studies* (pp. 130–146). Sage

Haslam, S. A., Reicher, S. D., & Birney, M. E. (2014). Nothing by mere authority: Evidence that in an experimental analogue of the Milgram paradigm participants are motivated not by orders but by appeals to science. *Journal of Social Issues, 70,* 473–488. https://doi.org/10.1111/josi.12072

Haslam, S. A., Reicher, S. D., & Millard, K. (2015). Shock treatment: Using immersive digital realism to restage and re-examine Milgram's 'obedience to authority' research. *PLoS One, 10*(3), e109015. https://doi.org/10.1371/journal.pone.0109015

Haslam, S. A., Reicher, S. D., Millard, K., & McDonald, R. (2015). 'Happy to have been of service': The Yale archive as a window into the engaged followership of participants in Milgram's 'obedience' experiments. *British Journal of Social Psychology, 54*(1), 55–83. https://doi.org/10.1111/bjso.12074

Haslam, S. A., Reicher, S. D., & Van Bavel, J. J. (2019). Rethinking the nature of cruelty: The role of identity leadership in the Stanford Prison Experiment. *American Psychologist, 74*(7), 809–822. https://doi.org/10.1037/amp0000443

Jetten, J., & Hornsey, M. J. (2017). Conformity: Revisiting Asch's line judgement studies. In J. R. Smith & S. A. Haslam (Eds.), *Social psychology: Revisiting the classic studies* (pp. 77–91). Sage

Latané, B., & Darley, J. M. (1968). Group inhibition of bystander intervention in emergencies. *Journal of Personality and Social Psychology, 10*(3), 215–221. https://doi.org/10.1037/h0026570

Latané, B., & Darley, J. M. (1970). *The unresponsive bystander: Why doesn't he help?* Appleton-Century-Crofts.

Latané, B., & Nida, S. (1981). Ten years of research on group size and helping. *Psychological Bulletin, 89*(2), 308–324. https://doi.org/10.1037/0033-2909.89.2.308

Le Texier, T. (2018). *Histoire d'un Mensonge: Enquête Sur L'Experience de Stanford.* Zones

Levine, M. (2017). Helping in emergencies: Revisiting Latane and Darley's bystander studies. In J. R. Smith & S. A. Haslam (Eds.), *Social psychology: Revisiting the classic studies* (pp. 201–217). Sage

Levine, M., & Crowther, S. (2008). The responsive bystander: How social group membership and group size can encourage as well as inhibit bystander intervention. *Journal of Personality and Social Psychology, 95*(6), 1429–1439. https://doi.org/10.1037/a0012634

Levine, M., Prosser, A., Evans, D., & Reicher, S. (2005). Identity and emergency intervention: How social group membership and inclusiveness of group boundaries shape helping behavior. *Personality and Social Psychology Bulletin, 31*(4), 443–453. https://doi.org/10.1177/0146167204271651

Manning, R., Levine, M., & Collins, A. (2007). The Kitty Genovese murder and the social psychology of helping: The parable of the 38 witnesses. *American Psychologist, 62*(6), 555. http://doi.org/10.1037/0003-066X.62.6.555

Milgram, S. (1963). Behavioral study of obedience. *Journal of Abnormal and Social Psychology, 67*, 371–378. https://doi.org/10.1037/h0040525

Milgram, S. (1974). *Obedience to authority: An experimental view.* Harper & Row

Philpot, R., Liebst, L. S., Levine, M., Bernasco, W., & Lindegaard, M. R. (2019). Would I be helped? Cross-national CCTV footage shows that intervention is the norm in public conflicts. *American Psychologist.* http:// doi.org/10.1037/amp0000469

Reicher, S., & Haslam, S. A. (2006). Rethinking the psychology of tyranny: The BBC prison study. *British Journal of Social Psychology, 45*, 1–40. https://doi.org/10.1348/014466605X48998

Reicher, S., & Haslam, S. A. (2011). After shock? Towards a social identity explanation of the Milgram 'obedience' studies. *British Journal of Social Psychology, 50*(1), 163–169. https://doi.org/10.1111/j.2044-8309.2010.02015.x

Reicher, S. D., Haslam, S. A., & Smith, J. R. (2012). Working toward the experimenter: Reconceptualizing obedience within the Milgram paradigm as identification-based followership. *Perspectives on Psychological Science, 7*, 315–324. http://doi.org/10.1177/1745691612448482

Rohrer, J. H., Baron, S. H., Hoffman, E. L., & Swander, D. V. (1954). The stability of autokinetic judgments. *The Journal of Abnormal and Social Psychology, 49*(4, Pt. 1), 595–597. https://doi.org/10.1037/h0060827

Sherif, M. (1935). A study of some social factors in perception. *Archives of Psychology (Columbia University), 187*, 60.

Sherif, M. (1936). *The psychology of social norms.* Harper

Sprong, S., Jetten, J., Wang, Z., Peters, K., Mols, F., Verkuyten, M., … & Badea, C. (2019). "Our country needs a strong leader right now": Economic inequality enhances the wish for a strong leader. *Psychological Science, 30*(11), 1625–1637. https://doi.org/10.1177/0956797619875472

Zimbardo, P. (1971). The psychological power and pathology of imprisonment. *Hearings before Subcommittee No. 3 of the Committee on the Judiciary House of Representatives Ninety-Second Congress, First sessions on corrections – Part II, Prisons, prison reform and prisoners' rights: California* (Serial No. 15, 25 October). Washington, DC: US Government Printing Office

Zimbardo, P. (2007). *The Lucifer effect: How good people turn evil.* Random House

Zimbardo, P. G. (2004). A situationist perspective on the psychology of evil: Understanding how good people are transformed into perpetrators. In A. Miller (Ed.), *The social psychology of good and evil* (pp. 21–50). Guilford

THE SELF AND INTERGROUP RELATIONS

Everywhere we look there are examples of group conflict. In school, we might notice that students form cliques based on common interests such as sports or fashion and that membership to these can feel exclusive. At work, we might notice tensions between different departments within the organisation or that the relationship between management and workers is strained. When we get home, all we have to do is turn on the news to see a plethora of examples of group conflict, whether it is countries at war, clashes between protestors and the police, or rising tensions between governments.

Why is the world so rife with group conflict? And given the destruction it can have, what can we do about it? These questions are part of an important area in psychology known as *intergroup relations*. In this chapter, we explore where conflict comes from, how it is handled by groups, and what we can do to encourage amicable intergroup relationships. Unfortunately, scientists are a long way from having the answers to these questions. However, given the influence groups have on who we are, it is not surprising that identity shapes how groups interact. Indeed, social identity theory is primarily a theory of intergroup conflict (Tajfel & Turner, 1979). As discussed in Chapter 3, the minimal group studies that underly social identity theory demonstrate that even when groups are random and meaningless, people favour their own group over other groups (Tajfel et al., 1971). What's more is that people were less interested in gaining the most benefit for their group than they were in ensuring that what they did get was better than what the other group got. In other words, doing better than the out-group was more important than the in-group doing well.

DOI: 10.4324/9780429274534-5

The minimal group studies offer two lessons for understanding the relationship between groups. The first is that simply being part of a group, even a group with no meaning, is the only criterion needed for members to show in-group favouritism. The second is that people are less motivated by personal gain than they are by group gains, establishing the inextricable link between people's self-concept and their membership to groups. Both points lay a foundation for understanding how groups relate to one another. However, it is important to remember that most groups *are* meaningful to their members and that their relationships with other groups *are* shaped by social context and complex histories. Hence, how groups treat and relate to each other is personal as well as social.

In this chapter, we consider how self-concept and identity shape and maintain the way groups perceive and treat each other. Central to these processes are stereotypes, prejudice, and discrimination. Often, these terms are used interchangeably when they are actually very different. In short, *stereotypes* are beliefs or opinions about a person based on their group membership, *prejudice* is a feeling about that person, and *discrimination* consists of (usually negative) actions or behaviours directed at someone based on these beliefs and feelings. Let's look at an example: Paul is a vegetarian who believes that people who eat meat don't care about the environment. When he meets James, who eats meat, he does not like him because of this. Paul is also a supervisor where James works. When James applies for a promotion, Paul does not consider his application. In this scenario, Paul's assumption that James doesn't care about the environment is a stereotype, his dislike of him is prejudice, and his unfair treatment of James is discrimination.

In the sections that follow, we will consider these processes in more depth, exploring how they develop and affect group dynamics. We will also focus on the consequences of these for marginalised groups and offer some suggestions for how intergroup relations might be improved.

STEREOTYPES

Stereotypes are exaggerated beliefs about people based on their group membership. These beliefs can be positive (e.g., Asians are good at math) or negative (e.g., overweight people are lazy) and can refer to people's personalities, attitudes, and behaviours. Psychologists consider stereotypes to be a form of cognitive shortcut that Gordon Allport famously described as the 'law of least effort' (Allport, 1954; also see our discussion of schemas in Chapter 1). Because it is impossible to carefully consider all the stimuli we are presented with on a daily basis, we make quick assumptions based on the little information we have available. As an example, think about the last time you saw a flying animal in your garden. Unless you know enough about these creatures to differentiate between them, you may have categorised them based on their overarching category as a bird rather than by their individual type (e.g., a chaffinch or a carrion crow).

The quick categorising of the stimuli around us forms the basis for stereotypes; rather than considering people's individual merits, we categorise each other based on the information we have immediate access to (e.g., race, gender, age), assumptions associated with these, and the environment we are in. The conclusions we make are based on perceptions so ingrained in our psyche, and judgements happen so quickly, that we may give little thought as to whether they are actually accurate. This helps account for why we might assume that the well-dressed White man in a corporate office is the boss, question the female doctor's competence, or think we sense danger when passing a Black man on the street. While quick judgements might be necessary to function in a world overloaded with stimuli, the above examples demonstrate the consequences they have for our attitudes (e.g., having respect for the 'boss,' distrust in the doctor, and fear from the man passing us) and, by extension, our behaviours (e.g., stepping out of the way so the 'boss' can pass, questioning the doctor's advice, clutching our valuables). Although these actions may seem subtle, they have important consequences for their targets. For instance, your concern about the female doctor's ability is something she may pick up on, fuelling her feelings of inadequacy. Your fear of the Black man contributes to his feelings of marginalisation. However, your assumption of the White male's status is likely to go unnoticed due to his privilege in that context (we will discuss this in more detail later in this chapter).

Importantly, because who we are is commensurate with our group membership, these examples are intergroup as much as they are interpersonal. Going back to our examples, your deference to the well-dressed White man may help reinforce the status quo within that organisation. Your questioning of the female doctor might contribute towards her decision to leave her field. Your clutching of your valuables may add to existing racial tensions in the community. To understand how this happens, it is important to think about these actions on a group level. That is, instead of considering the effects of your actions alone, imagine that most people in your group acted in the same way. As a case in point, if you consider that a large portion of the female doctor's patients question her competence, it may be easier to see why women drop out of medicine at higher rates than men (see Hertz-Tang & Carnes, 2020).

Perhaps a natural reaction to thinking about how we stereotype and the harm it causes is guilt. After all, most of us don't intend to hurt others. However, it's important that we recognise that one of the most harmful things we can do for intergroup relations is to become defensive or deny our stereotypes. Instead, we need to understand that everybody stereotypes others and that often it happens without us realising we are doing it. Remember that stereotyping is a cognitive shortcut that is, in many respects, necessary for us to function. An inherent part of this process is that we will make mistakes and categorise others incorrectly. The tendency for this to happen largely outside of our consciousness is known as *implicit bias*. What makes these biases so dangerous is that they are often not in line with our self-concept and may even be at odds with our own values. For instance, a teacher may believe strongly that everyone should have equal opportunities but at the same time have an implicit bias that students of colour are less academically inclined than White students. Although she does not realise it, the result of this bias is that she calls on her White students more than her students of colour, an action that reduces learning opportunities for the latter (Holroyd et al., 2017).

Where do these implicit biases come from? And how it is possible that we can have such differing explicit and implicit beliefs? The answer comes largely from the fact that stereotypes are culturally shared and historically rooted. As discussed in Chapter 2, who we are has been shaped by the social world that we've grown up in and lived. Hence, we are all part of a system that internalises and then perpetuates certain beliefs. Using racism as an example, changing social norms has meant that self-reported racist beliefs have declined, while implicit bias in favour of White people remains prevalent (Hofmann et al., 2005). In the case of our teacher, her implicit bias against her students of colour may, in part, be due to a history of slavery and the fact that people of colour continue to be portrayed negatively in the media. In fact, research has found that implicit biases against Black Americans are strongest in the U.S. countries that were more dependent on slaves in 1860 (Payne et al., 2019), demonstrating the importance that historical contexts can have on the categorisations we make. Hence, our teacher is demonstrating biases that many White Americans have about Black Americans – often without even realising it.

However, just because we may not always be aware of our biases does not absolve us of responsibility for them. The key is to learn to recognise and challenge them. To better understand where these implicit biases come from, we turn our attention to evidence of the magnitude in which stereotyped beliefs permeate our society.

BOX 5.1   REAL-WORLD APPLICATION

One strategy to reduce implicit biases is to raise the frequency in which people are exposed to counter-stereotypical images, stories, and examples (Lai et al., 2013). Sean Williams, founder of 'The Dad Gang,' has sought to do just that. Even though Black fathers are more involved in their children's daily lives than White and Hispanic dads (Jones & Mosher, 2013), the myth of the 'missing black father' prevails. To combat this stereotype, Williams started a movement to change perceptions of Black fathers, largely through candid images of Black fatherhood that he shares through social media. You can find out more at www.thedadgang.com.

STEREOTYPE CONTENT

The research on implicit bias demonstrates the power stereotypes have to shape intergroup relations. But, while ideas about social groups are deeply rooted within our culture, it is not always obvious where we learn them from, especially if we can't remember being taught them. This is because stereotypes form part of our *social cognitions*; how we process, remember, and use information within our social world (Fiske & Taylor, 2013). These cognitions are learned from a young age and reinforced as we grow up. For instance, children learn gender stereotypes through the toys they are encouraged to play with (e.g., toy cars for boys and toy kitchens for girls; Blakemore, 2003), how adults interact with them (e.g., rough play with boys and discussing emotions with girls; Golombok & Fivush, 1994), and even chores they are given [e.g., boys helping with do-it-yourself (DIY) jobs and girls helping with housework; see Meeussen et al., 2020]. Norms around how genders should behave are then internalised, and by the time children become young adults, they tend to imagine their futures in line with gender stereotypes (Meeussen et al., 2016). Research has shown that at the age of six, girls are less likely than boys to believe that adults of their gender are 'brilliant,' a belief that can shape their interests and, eventually, their career choices (Bian et al., 2017).

Because of this cyclical relationship – where stereotypes shape reality and then reality perpetuates stereotypes – stereotypes are difficult to change. As such, they can remain relatively stable for generations. In 1933, researchers gave White male Princeton University students 84 traits and asked them to select the 5 they felt were the most typical of different ethnic groups in the U.S. In some respects, the study could have taken place yesterday: Jews were described as shrewd, industrious, and intelligent, while Italians were described as impulsive, passionate, and quick-tempered. In a replication of the study, Madon and colleagues (2001) found that negative stereotypes of African Americans from 1933 had remained largely consistent throughout the 20th century (e.g., superstitious, lazy, ignorant).

Despite this tendency to remain stable, change is certainly not impossible. Structural changes within a society and increased contact between members of different groups can help stereotypes evolve (Madon et al., 2001). As a case in point, gender stereotypes state that men embody *agentic traits* (e.g., ambitious, assertive, dominant) and women embody *communal traits* (e.g., warm, compassionate, willing to share emotions; Sczesny et al., 2019). However, as women have gained access to traditionally male domains, perceptions of women as agentic have started to increase. For men, there has been less progress in their access to traditionally female roles, and, as such, traditional stereotypes about men have largely remained stable (see Wilde & Diekman, 2005). Furthermore, in the 2001 replication of the 1933 Princeton study mentioned above, researchers found that group stereotypes tended to become more favourable rather than less over time (Madon et al., 2001).

It is important to note that even favourable stereotypes put target groups at a disadvantage. Let's look again at gender stereotypes. Stereotypes of women as communal mean that they are generally perceived more positively than men. However, these likeable characteristics also tend to be seen as inappropriate for leadership roles. As such, women who do reach high levels on the corporate ladder often face discrimination for acting similarly to their male colleagues (Eagly & Karau, 2002). On the other hand, the less likeable attributes associated with agentic traits mean that men tend to face discrimination when working in roles that require helping or care (e.g., nursing, stay-at-home dad; see Meeussen et al., 2020). Although an influx of women to the work force over the past 75 years has increased the view that women and men are equally competent, overall perceptions of women as communal and perceptions of men as agentic remain strong (Eagly et al., 2020).

At a basic level, the stereotype that women are communal while men are agentic is that what is viewed as appropriate for each gender limits people to only half of the qualities that make us human. Not only does this have consequences for our self-concept, it shapes the challenges we face at a group level. For instance, research has shown that death rates among men are over 200% higher than women, a statistic that can be largely explained by the poorer physical and mental self-care exhibited by men who see such behaviours as 'feminine' (Meeussen et al., 2020). For women, stereotypes around femininity have economic disadvantages. Data shows that, overall, White women made $0.81 for every dollar made by White men, with this disparity rising for women of colour (Payscale, 2020). Although the reasons for this gap are complex, it is clear from the research that stereotypes play a role; Eagly and Karau (2002) found that when the stereotypes associated with an employee's group membership is inconsistent with their role (e.g., women in roles that require agency, men in roles that require communion), they received poorer performance evaluations.

The classification of people based on whether they are communal or agentic is not limited to gender. According to the *stereotype content model*, most stereotypes about groups contain two underlying elements: warmth and competence (Fiske et al., 2002). Groups are considered competent to the extent that they are perceived as powerful and high in status, while groups are considered warm to the extent that they do not compete with others. The theory states that how groups fall along each continuum impacts on others' perceptions them. For example, the elderly (low in competence but high in warmth) tend to be treated with paternalism, while homeless people and welfare recipients (low competence and low warmth) tend to be treated with contempt. Those perceived as high in competence but low in warmth (i.e., rich people) are viewed with envy, while those high in both competence and warmth (i.e., the middle class) tend to be admired (Fiske et al., 2002).

Stereotypes play a vital role in our social world, affecting our self-concept and group identity. Every group identity we have is subject to stereotypes. While both positive and negative stereotypes have the potential to be problematic for groups, we know that marginalised groups in society are particularly vulnerable to the disadvantages brought by stereotypes. In the next section, we turn our attention away from the content of stereotypes and focus on the consequences of stereotypes.

CONSEQUENCES OF STEREOTYPES

Because stereotypes are culturally shared, *all* people within a society are usually familiar with them. This includes their targets. In addition to being aware of how their group is perceived, targets of stereotypes can internalise these beliefs. Hence, stereotypes serve to justify and then perpetuate social stigmas (Biernat & Dovidio, 2000). According to Goffman (1963), a *stigma* is an attribute that discredits an individual by marking them in a way that reduces them 'from a whole and usual person to a discounted one.' These marks can take many forms and can include aspects of one's appearance (e.g., facial deformity), behaviour (e.g., sexual deviance), and group membership (e.g., immigrant; Major & O'brien, 2005). Because people with stigmatised identities must contend with the stereotypes associated with these identities every day, the two can easily become entwined. As a result, people who experience stigma may devalue their own identities.

One powerful example of internalised stigmas can be found in Kenneth and Mamie Clark's classic doll studies. The studies were conducted in the 1940s using 253 African American preschool children, the majority of whom attended segregated schools. The children were presented with two dolls that were identical except for their skin colour (one had brown skin and one had white skin). They were then asked questions about which doll was 'good' and 'bad,' which they preferred to play with, and which they thought looked like them. Overwhelmingly, the white doll was preferred over the black doll; two thirds of the children stated that they liked the white doll 'best' and that it was the 'nice doll.' Nearly 60% stated that the black doll 'looks bad' and the majority picked the white doll to play with. Some of the children became so distraught when asked to identify the doll that was like them; they cried and had to leave the room (Clark & Clark, 1947). Based on this data and other work, the researchers concluded that "it is clear that the Negro child, by the age of five, is aware of the fact that to be coloured in contemporary American society is a mark of inferior status" (Clark & Clark, 1950).

While it may be easy to dismiss the results of the doll experiments as representative of the segregated 1940s, follow-up studies demonstrate that these beliefs are still ingrained in our thinking today. In 2010, American television channel CNN ran their own version of the study by asking both Black and White children to rate cartoon characters of varying skin colours. Their results showed that while both races preferred the lighter skinned characters, this preference was particularly pronounced among White children. Overall, positive beliefs were attributed to lighter skin, while negative beliefs were attributed to darker skin (CNN, 2010). In another follow-up study, Byrd and colleagues (2017) found that in a sample of 50 children (98% of whom were African American), preferences were similar to the original doll experiments: when asked which doll was the 'nice doll,' the majority chose the white doll, and, when asked which doll was 'mean,' the darker-skinned doll was chosen. The researchers also varied the texture of the dolls' hair. As expected, the children preferred the doll with long straight hair, reflecting societal beliefs that 'white' hair is more beautiful than 'black' hair (see Byrd et al., 2017).

The internalisation of stereotypes demonstrates that stigma threatens targets' self-concept: people don't know if how they are being treated is due to their behaviour or whether it's a response to their stigmatised identity (Crocker et al., 1998). Compounding this is a phenomenon known as *stereotype threat*, which occurs when a person's fear of confirming negative stereotypes about their group impedes their performance on stigma-related tasks (Steele & Aronson, 1995). Psychologists coined the term after finding that Black students only performed worse than White students on academic tests when they were told it was diagnostic of their intellectual ability, an instruction that activated the stereotype that Black people are less intellectually capable than White people. When they changed the instruction to become non-threatening (the test was simply a problem-solving task that did not indicate ability), performance differences between White and Black students disappeared. The researchers concluded that because the Black students receiving the threatening instructions were fearful of confirming negative stereotypes about their group, the instruction created a cognitive burden that prevented them from performing to their full potential (Steele & Aronson, 1995).

Over 300 experiments have evidenced the impact stereotype threat has on performance. Reminders of negative stereotypes have been shown to impair women's performance on math tests (relative to men; Spencer et al., 1999), older people's performance on memory tests (relative to young people; Hess & Hinson, 2006), and White men's athletic ability (relative to Black men; Stone, 2002), to name but a few. However, stereotype threat goes beyond impacting our ability to perform on tests. An environment can activate stereotype threat if there are cues in the setting that heighten people's awareness of the negative stereotypes attached to their group (Murphy et al., 2007). These include anything that sends the message that one's social group does not belong within a given domain (Lewis & Sekaquaptewa, 2016). For example, a woman who enters an all-male office may be vulnerable to stereotype threat because the absence of other women signals that within this environment, women are not capable of success.

The experience of stigma is not limited to the internalisation of negative stereotypes; people with stigmatised identities must also contend with discrimination that can occur rarely (e.g., hate crimes), chronically (e.g., bullying), and as part of everyday life (e.g., poorer service; see Frost, 2011). Because of these experiences, stigmatised individuals may come to expect discrimination and, to cope with this, may attempt to manage their stigma as a way of self-protection (Barreto, 2015). Depending on whether the stigma is visible or not, this can take the form of concealing the stigma or attempting to manage others' reactions to the stigma (for instance, by altering any behaviours, mannerisms, or language the stigma is associated with). As an example, a non-native speaker might feel stigmatised by their non-native accent. To cope with this, they might avoid conversations with native speakers where possible or attempt to conceal their accent by imitating native speech (Birney et al., 2020). For those who can't or don't want to hide their stigma completely, they might take the approach of drawing attention away from their stigma. For instance, a woman who feels stigmatised because of her weight might make a point of showing off her witty sense of humour (Miller et al., 1995).

All these strategies have consequences for interpersonal and intergroup relations. On the one hand, revealing a stigma risks discrimination, a consequence that has negative repercussions for the individual while also increasing group-based tensions (Barreto, 2015). On the other hand, hiding a stigma impairs the quality of social interactions due to the anxiety around being discovered and the feeling that a relationship is inauthentic (Newheiser & Barreto, 2014). These consequences have adverse effects on individuals' overall well-being and self-confidence (Barreto et al., 2006). Furthermore, avoiding situations, people, and environments limits opportunities for stigmatised groups while also contributing to maintenance of the status quo: if non-stigmatised groups are not confronted with people with stigmatised identities, their stereotypes about them are unlikely to change (Barreto, 2015). Finally, drawing attention away from one's stigma during intergroup interactions can affect groups differently. While positive interactions might improve the attitudes of non-stigmatised people, they are cognitively depleting and can feel disingenuous for those on the receiving end of stigma.

It is important to note that while any group can be stereotyped, the experience of stigma is only relevant for low-status groups. Because high-status groups benefit from their group membership and tend to hold positions of power, they are unlikely to perceive instances of stereotyping or even discrimination as indicative of their abilities or life chances. Such instances are also less likely to reflect pervasive discrimination like that experienced by low-status groups (Schmitt et al., 2002). Furthermore, high-status groups do not have the cognitive burdens of continuously anticipating negative evaluations or of having to manage the reactions of out-group members. For these reasons, stereotypes have different consequences depending on group status. This helps to explain why, in the context of race, for example, a Black person negatively stereotyping a White person does not harm the White person in the same way that the Black person is harmed when the situation is reversed. Stigma only exists when unequal power dynamics allow for labelling, negative stereotyping, exclusion, and discrimination to target low-status groups (Major & O'brien, 2005).

It is also important to keep in mind that because we have multiple identities, some identities can be stigmatised, while others allow us to benefit from unequal power dynamics. For example, a White woman with a disability may be stigmatised in contexts where her gender or her disability is salient. Yet, at the same time, her race gives her an advantage in a world that advantages White people. We will discuss this privilege in more detail later in this chapter. Before we do, we turn our attention to key outcomes of stereotypes that play a vital role in shaping the relationship between groups: prejudice and discrimination.

BOX 5.2   REFLECT

1   Think about your various social identities.
2   Write down your race, gender, transgender status, and sexuality.
3   Ask yourself:
    Which identities on your list are stigmatised and which are not?
    How do you cope with your stigmatised identities?
    Thinking about your privileged identities, how aware are you of
        others whose identities are stigmatised? What could you do
        to help ensure they feel safe from stigma?

PREJUDICE AND INTERGROUP RELATIONS

Although prejudice and discrimination are distinct concepts, they tend to go hand in hand. Importantly, discrimination is often a result of prejudice. As such, we will discuss them as one in this section. In line with Brown (2011), we use the following definition for prejudice: Any attitude, emotion, or behaviour towards members of a group, which directly or indirectly implies some negativity or antipathy towards that group.

Prejudice is, perhaps, the most influential factor in shaping intergroup relations. At best, it is a driver of stigma and inequality. At worst, it results in *genocide*, the extermination of an entire social group. As discussed in the previous section, the former is as pervasive in society as it is damaging. The latter, unfortunately, is more prevalent than most of us would like to believe: the extermination of over 6 million Jews by the Nazi regime (1941–1945), 2 million Cambodians during the rule of the Khmer Rouge (1975–1979), and 70% of Rwandan Tutsis by the Hutu majority (1994) are just a few examples of the genocides that have occurred in modern times. Whatever form it takes, prejudice appears to be a part of every human society. Groups have been killing each other since the beginning of time, and explicit prejudicial beliefs in the form that we would recognise today have been traced back as early as the 16th century (LaPiere & Farnsworth, 1949).

Just as every society is plagued by prejudice, so is every social group. However, some groups are more vulnerable to and affected by prejudice than others because of their status within the social context they are in. While not the only forms, main areas of prejudice include gender (i.e., sexism), race (i.e., racism), age (i.e., age-ism), sexuality (e.g., sexualism), and ability (e.g., ableism). Prejudice can be overt (openly expressing negative attitudes or behaviours towards specific groups) or covert (hiding negative group-based attitudes and concealing discriminatory acts). While both are experienced by marginalised groups, overt prejudice has fallen, largely due to social norms that stress the importance of equal rights and treatment for all. Covert prejudice, on the other hand, remains prevalent in nearly every part of society (Hutchings & Sullivan, 2019).

Although there is no doubt that overt prejudice is harmful, there are some ways in which covert prejudice is more dangerous. This is due to the difficulty around detecting it, recognising it, and therefore preventing it. Covert prejudice occurs when there is a failure to support or provide access to a social group, resulting in exclusion of that group from parts of society. This might take the form of planners failing to provide wheelchair access in a building or employers removing important projects from their pregnant workers. In these situations, such decisions may be attributed to seemingly innocent reasoning (e.g., financial considerations, kindness) making them difficult to contest. Another example of covert prejudice is when high-status groups engage in *tokenism*, defined as a positive but relatively trivial act that benefits a minority group. Although the act might seem supportive of inclusion, it can be used as reason for not making any of the meaningful change that is necessary for genuine equality. A typical example of tokenism is when an organisation hires a minority group member and then uses the appointment to deflect accusations of prejudicial hiring overall (Konrad et al., 2008).

The distinction between overt prejudice and covert prejudice, and the trend towards the latter, is illustrated by *ambivalent sexism theory* (Glick & Fiske, 1996). According to this theory, sexist attitudes consist of two distinct but related concepts that perpetuate gender inequality: hostile and benevolent sexism. *Hostile sexism* is generally overt and is characterised by a dislike of women based on the belief that they seek to abolish men's power. *Benevolent sexism* is the belief that women are uniquely placed to provide care and support to men but are incompetent and in need of protection (Glick & Fiske, 1996). Benevolent sexism is an example of covert prejudice because it is so subtle that it can seem flattering. Examples of benevolent sexist beliefs include notions of women as inherently nurturing and beautiful. These seemingly innocent attitudes play an important role in maintaining women's lack of power in society in comparison with men. For example, the belief that women are natural caregivers rationalises their over-representation in care roles that leave them dependent on men as economic providers. Likewise, the idea that women are beautiful advances notions that women's worth is measured by appearance rather than by skill or intellect (Glick & Fiske, 1996). Benevolent sexism also appears to be particularly tenacious; in contrast to hostile sexism which has been shown to decrease as men age, men's endorsement of benevolent sexism remains relatively consistent throughout their lives (Hammond et al., 2018).

The issue of covert prejudice should not trivialise the consequences of overt prejudice. Indeed, one of the most overt forms of prejudice is also one of the most troubling: *hate crimes*. These crimes are broadly defined as those where the victim has been targeted because of their real or perceived membership to a social group. While the social group targeted can vary, it is usually based on race, nationality, religion, disability, sexual orientation, and gender identity. Some police departments have expanded the groups recognised as hate-crime victims to include subcultures (e.g., Emos or Goths; BBC, 2015). Hate crimes themselves can take a variety of forms, ranging from verbal abuse to murder. In terms of the crime committed, hate crimes can look identical to other crimes. What makes them distinct is that they are motivated by bias against a person because of the social group they belong to. As a result, hate crimes go beyond hurting the victim by terrorising the victim's community. For example, an unfortunately common instance of islamophobia (e.g., hatred of Muslims) is to verbally abuse women wearing head coverings in public spaces. Not only does this traumatise the victim, but instances like this can lead all Muslim women to fear similar experiences. Research looking at hate crimes against members of the LGBTQ+ community found that just knowing about an in-group member who had experienced a hate crime was enough to instil feelings of threat from out-group members (Paterson et al., 2019).

Hate crimes also have important implications for intergroup relations. In addition to feeling threatened by those outside of their group, both victims and their fellow group members might alter their behaviours when a hate crime occurs; feelings of anger can lead to more proactive behaviours (e.g., joining anti-hate groups), while feelings of anxiety can lead to more avoidance behaviours (e.g., staying away from certain people or places; Paterson et al., 2019). The former might result in more visibility of the group's plight, while the latter can result in targeted groups internalising stigma. Furthermore, how group members relate to hate-crime victims have repercussions for their group identity. Research has shown that group members who have personal experiences with hate crimes are more likely to victim-blame, while those only aware of the hate crime are more likely to express empathy for victims (Paterson et al., 2019). These reactions are important because whether group members can come together helps determine the group's ability to act collectively against hate.

Whether prejudice takes the form of tokenism or a hate crime, these attitudes and behaviours not only harm individual victims but have consequences for social groups. But why does prejudice happen? And what makes prejudice so ingrained in our social world? Social identity theory offers some intriguing insights into these questions.

A SOCIAL IDENTITY PERSPECTIVE OF PREJUDICE AND INTERGROUP RELATIONS

There are many theories that aim to explain the existence of prejudice. Some of these focus on personality (e.g., social dominance orientation, authoritarian personality trait), others focus on cognition (e.g., dogmatism), while others consider parental influence, innate biases, and competing group interests. In their own way, each of these theories contributes to the way we understand and conceptualise prejudice. In this section, we focus on understanding prejudice using a social identity approach, which sees prejudice as evolving out of group processes. From this perspective, prejudice is the result of a person's individual characteristics mattering less than their group markers. Furthermore, prejudice depends on status: who prejudice harms and who benefits from prejudiced societies are determined by the power dynamics that exist between groups (see Brown, 2011). Hence, to understand the scale of prejudice and its role within societies, it is important to see prejudice as a group-based phenomenon rather than something that occurs between individuals. This section, in line with Brown (2011), will give an overview of three aspects of social identity theory that offer insight into prejudice: intergroup similarity, group status relations, and group identification.

One question that has puzzled scientists and laypeople alike is that it often seems that the groups who hate each other the most tend to be the most alike. For example, conflict between Serbians and Croatians resulted in tens of thousands of deaths despite these groups sharing the same language and culture. Fighting between Catholics and Protestants in Northern Ireland went on for decades even though differences between them were indistinguishable to most outsiders (Nagle & Clancy, 2010). Tensions between Sunni Muslims and Shia Muslims remain strong despite sharing the same overarching faith. While outsiders may perceive differences between these groups as trivial, they are deeply important to the groups involved. Indeed, some of the worst mass murders in history have been committed by nearly identical groups; in Rwanda, Hutus killed over 800,000 Tutsi over the course of 100 days, even though it wasn't always clear who was a Tutsi and who was a Hutu (Gwin, 2014). In 1917, Sigmund Freud famously described the hypersensitivity of similar groups to their differences as 'the narcissism of minor differences.'

While extreme brutality between similar groups might seem counter-intuitive, it is logical within a social identity framework. As discussed in Chapter 3, a main tenet of this theory is *positive distinctiveness*; we need to see the groups that we belong to more positively than the groups that we do not belong to (Tajfel & Turner, 1979). To achieve this, group members focus on the positive ways in which their group is different from the comparable out-group. To maintain a positive sense of self, it is vital that positive differences remain *distinct* from other groups. Without it, it would be impossible to differentiate between groups, and the group's identity would lose its meaning. Hence, out-groups that are too similar to us threaten our positive distinctiveness and, by extension, our self-concept. According to social identity theory, it is for this reason that miniscule differences between similar groups become immensely important. As an explanation for prejudice, a strength of this approach is its ability to help explain the hatred that we see between groups that seemingly have the most in common.

Another contribution of the social identity approach is its focus on in-group bias and status. As discussed in the sections above, some groups have more power and greater access to resources than others. In Chapter 3, I outlined a range of strategies that low-status groups employ to cope with their position, from joining the high-status out-group to fighting for social change. High-status groups, however, tend to manage their position by favouring their own group. As Scheepers and colleagues (2006) point out, one function of in-group bias is to confirm one's social reality. Hence, groups that are high in status will be particularly motivated to favour their own group as doing so both affirms and cements their socially defined superiority (Brown, 2011). This could take several forms, from preferring the in-group job candidate to being more polite to the shop assistant with membership to the same high-status social group.

Perhaps a fair criticism of this perspective is that in-group favouritism does not equate to out-group derogation. Indeed, hiring the in-group candidate over a similarly qualified out-group candidate is not on par with committing a hate crime. But as Molina and colleagues (2016) point out, favouring one's group does contribute towards out-group hate. More specifically, when in-group bias occurs in conjunction with other factors, for instance, perceived out-group threat or group norms that legitimise harmful treatment of certain groups, the result is out-group degradation. Other research has found that detecting changes to the status quo is particularly stressful for high-status groups, likely because they have the most to lose from change (see Jetten et al., 2017). Supporting this idea, Scheepers and colleagues (2009) found that high-status group members who detect such changes exhibit a physiological stress response (e.g., higher blood pressure) and are more likely to make prejudicial statements about the out-group when around fellow in-group members. Hence, high-status groups' tendency to favour their in-group makes an important contribution to the existence of prejudice.

Finally, how strongly group members identify with their respective groups can offer insight into the processes that lead to prejudice. According to social identity theory, a person's sense of self is inextricably tied to their group identity; that is, the goals, successes, and failures of one's group become synonymous with one's personal goals, successes, and failures (Tajfel & Turner, 1979). The extent to which this is the case (i.e., how strongly one *identifies* with their group) helps determine the strength of their prejudices. However, the relationship between identification and prejudice is not direct (Brown, 2011). Rather, research suggests that identification acts as an amplifier of more direct causes of prejudice. Research by Brown and colleagues (2001) illustrates this point nicely. Data was collected from British passengers while travelling to France via ferry over two days. On one of the days, French fishermen had blockaded the port causing delays (high intergroup conflict), and on the other day, there was no such blockade and travel went smoothly (low intergroup conflict). On the day where intergroup conflict was high, negative stereotypes about the French were evident among high and moderate identifiers but negligible among low identifiers (Brown et al., 2001). In other words, participants who identified more as British were more prone to prejudice when perceiving conflict between their group and the French fishermen. However, for minority group members, the relationship between identification and prejudice may be more direct. For instance, highly identified minority group members tend to report more instances of prejudice, possibly because majority group members detect this and then treat them more negatively (Kaiser & Wilkins, 2010).

While no psychological theory can explain prejudice completely, social identity theory can offer insights into how prejudice evolves and the consequences it has for intergroup relations. However, rather than being a theoretical exercise, a reason for extending our knowledge of prejudice is that we can learn how best to reduce it. In the section that follows, we turn our attention to the application of psychological theory to what is arguably one of its most important contributions: improving the relationship between groups.

IMPROVING INTERGROUP RELATIONS

Scholars have long suggested that to reduce prejudice and improve intergroup relations, members of different groups should interact with one another. Today, this hypothesis is known as *intergroup contact theory* (Allport, 1954). According to this idea, prejudice can be reduced if out-group members are brought together in certain conditions. First, members should be of *equal status* (e.g., employees of the same rank). Second, their environment should promote *cooperation* (e.g., students working on a group project). Third, they should share a *common goal* (e.g., a sports team vying for the championship title). All of this should ideally happen with support from relevant authority figures. Since Allport's (1954) hypothesis was first proposed, a wealth of research has demonstrated the effectiveness of intergroup contact. Although the benefits are greater when the four optimal conditions listed above are met, we know that prejudice can still be reduced if one or more of these are missing (Pettigrew & Tropp, 2006).

To be effective, intergroup contact does not have to be face to face. Reductions in prejudice have been shown after *extended contact* (i.e., an awareness of in-group members having out-group friends), *vicarious contact* (e.g., observing how an in-group member behaves around a member of the out-group), *imagined contact* (e.g., actively envisioning a positive interaction with an out-group member), and *virtual contact* (e.g., contact between group members over a computer; see Dovidio et al., 2017). Although the different forms vary in effectiveness (Lemmer & Wagner, 2015), they work by reducing anxiety about the out-group, promoting a common identity between members of different groups, and encouraging empathy for others (Pettigrew & Tropp, 2006). As more group members experience contact with an out-group, these benefits can alter *intra*-group norms that encourage less prejudice towards that out-group, further extending contact's benefits (see Dovidio, 2013). As such, intergroup contact theory is considered one of the most effective ways of improving the relationship between groups. In recent work looking at non-Black physicians over the course of their six-year training programme, intergroup contact was found to be more effective for reducing prejudice than other interventions with the same aim (e.g., diversity training; Onyeador et al., 2020).

However, the promise of contact to improve intergroup relations can be overshadowed by its capacity to backfire, harming out-group perceptions instead. According to Pettigrew and Tropp (2006), intergroup contact can exacerbate intergroup threat, depending on the type of contact experienced by group members. While *contact quality* (i.e., developing deep personal relationships) can reduce perceptions of out-group threat, *contact quantity* (i.e., the frequency of interactions) can amplify these. Let's take the example of immigrants and non-immigrants. Non-immigrants who only have frequent contact with immigrants may perceive the out-group's sizeable presence in their life as a threat to their group's identity and resources (Craig & Richeson, 2014). But if non-immigrants develop close friendships with immigrants, they are less likely to perceive this group as a threat, and prejudice against them can be reduced. Hence, it is important to keep in mind that not just any interaction between group members is beneficial. Rather, improving intergroup relations through contact requires interactions that are high in quality.

Perhaps a more worrying consequence when intergroup contact backfires is the potential it has to hinder equality. While it is promising that groups show reduced prejudice after quality contact, this does not necessarily translate to majority group members acting to eliminate discriminatory laws and practices. Furthermore, if minority groups have improved perceptions of the majority group, this can weaken their awareness of their comparative disadvantage. While research shows that the effects of intergroup contact are weaker for minority group members, positive interactions with members of the majority might make them less likely to challenge these groups for equal rights (Tropp & Pettigrew, 2005). Hence, intergroup contact results in a paradox; it can reduce prejudice while at the same time impeding real social change.

CONCLUSION

It is often thought that the most idyllic goal humans have is achieving world peace. Yet, this goal is also pegged as the world's most unrealistic; stamping out prejudice and discrimination seems unsurmountable and the complexities of intergroup relations impossible to untangle. However, viewing intergroup relations through the lens of social identity provides insight for overcoming these challenges. If we can recognise how our identities shape intergroup relations and likewise how intergroup relations shape our identities, we can take start to make change. One way to do this is by understanding how our own social identities perpetuate status differences and inequality. Most of us have at least one such *privileged* identity which give us an advantage in the social world we live in. For instance, a White person who is stopped by the police does not usually fear for their life the way a Black person is likely to, given the latter group's history with police brutality. This is a privilege. Men walking home after a night out do not usually fear sexual assault the way women do, given the latter's vulnerability in this if domain. This is also a privilege. The general rule on privilege is that if there is an experience that affects a group of people, but it's something that you don't have to think about; it's probably a privilege.

Privilege can be a contentious topic for people, but it really shouldn't be. Having privilege does not make you a bad person, nor is it something to feel guilty about. In fact, you can't 'opt' out of privilege even if you wanted to! What you can do is recognise the privilege you have and do what you can to level the playing field for others. Remember that it is necessary to view these ideas on a group level rather than on an individual one; a person can have a very difficult life in many ways but can still benefit from certain privileges depending on their social identities. Indeed, unequal societies depend on people benefiting from the expense of others, and as such, most of us are both targets and agents of this oppression system. Hence, if there is one thing that can be done to improve the relationship between groups (and get closer to the effusive goal of world peace!), it is to recognise and then challenge the privilege you have. In this way, all of us have a part to play in improving intergroup relations.

CHAPTER SUMMARY

- Stereotypes are culturally shared ideas based on beliefs about people's group memberships.
- We are often unaware of our biases against certain groups, making it vital that we learn to recognise and challenge them.
- The content of group stereotypes is difficult, though not impossible, to change.
- People with stigmatised social identities face a number of disadvantages and may try to manage others' responses to their stigma.
- Prejudice and discrimination are widespread, taking many different, and often subtle, forms.
- The social identity approach suggests that prejudice is driven by threats to positive distinctiveness and the in-group favouritism exhibited by high-status groups.
- While intergroup contact is an effective strategy for improving intergroup relations, it also has the potential to make them worse.

WANT TO KNOW MORE?

Recommended Reading:
- Brown, R., & Pehrson, S. (2019). *Group processes: Dynamics within and between groups*. John Wiley & Sons

REFERENCES

Allport, G. W. (1954). *The nature of prejudice*. Addison-Wesley

Barreto, M. (2015). Experiencing and coping with social stigma. In M. E. Mikulincer, P. R. Shaver, J. F. Dovidio & J. A. Simpson (Eds.), *APA handbook of personality and social psychology, Volume 2: Group processes* (pp. 473–506). American Psychological Association

Barreto, M., Ellemers, N., & Banal, S. (2006). Working under cover: Performance-related self-confidence among members of contextually devalued groups who try to pass. *European Journal of Social Psychology, 36*(3), 337–352. https://doi.org/10.1002/ejsp.314

BBC. (2015, November 25). *Subculture abuse classed as hate crime*. https://www.bbc.co.uk/news/uk-england-leicestershire-34919722

Bian, L., Leslie, S. J., & Cimpian, A. (2017). Gender stereotypes about intellectual ability emerge early and influence children's interests. *Science, 355*(6323), 389–391. http://doi.org/10.1126/science.aah6524

Biernat, M., & Dovidio, J. F. (2000). Stigma and stereotypes. In T. F. Heatherton, R. E. Kleck, M. R. Hebl, & J. G. Hull (Eds.), *The social psychology of stigma* (pp. 88–125). Guilford Press

Birney, M. E., Rabinovich, A., Morton, T. A., Heath, H., & Ashcroft, S. (2020). When speaking English is not enough: The consequences of language-based stigma for nonnative speakers. *Journal of Language and Social Psychology, 39*(1), 67–86. https://doi.org/10.1177/0261927X19883906

Blakemore, J. E. O. (2003). Children's beliefs about violating gender norms: Boys shouldn't look like girls, and girls shouldn't act like boys. *Sex Roles, 48*(9–10), 411–419. https://doi.org/10.1023/A:1023574427720

Brown, R. (2011). *Prejudice: Its social psychology*. John Wiley & Sons

Brown, R., Maras, P., Masser, B., Vivian, J., & Hewstone, M. (2001). Life on the ocean wave: Testing some intergroup hypotheses in a naturalistic setting. *Group Processes & Intergroup Relations, 4*(2), 81–97. https://doi.org/10.1177/1368430201004002001

Byrd, D., Ceacal, Y. R., Felton, J., Nicholson, C., Rhaney, D. M. L., McCray, N., & Young, J. (2017). A modern doll study: Self concept. *Race, Gender & Class, 24*(1/2), 186–202. https://search.proquest.com/docview/2119847048?accountid=14620

Clark, K. B., & Clark, M. P. (1947). Racial identification and preference in Negro children. In T. M. Newcomb & E. L. Hartley (Eds.), *Readings in social psychology* (pp. 169–178). Henry Holt

Clark, K., & Clark, M. (1950). Emotional factors in racial identification and preference in negro children. *The Journal of Negro Education, 19*(3), 341–350. https://doi.org/10.2307/2966491

CNN. (2010, May 14). *Study: White and Black children bias towards lighter skin*. https://edition.cnn.com/2010/US/05/13/doll.study/index.html

Craig, M. A., & Richeson, J. A. (2014). On the precipice of a "majority-minority" America: Perceived status threat from the racial demographic shift affects White Americans' political ideology. *Psychological Science, 25*(6), 1189–1197. https://doi.org/10.1177/0956797614527113

Crocker, J., Major, B., & Steele, C. (1998). Social stigma. In S. Fiske, D. Gilbert, & G. Lindzey (Eds.), *Handbook of social psychology* (Vol. 2, pp. 504–553). McGraw-Hill

Dovidio, J. F. (2013). Bridging intragroup processes and intergroup relations: Needing the twain to meet. *British Journal of Social Psychology, 52*(1), 1–24. https://doi.org/10.1111/bjso.12026

Dovidio, J. F., Love, A., Schellhaas, F. M., & Hewstone, M. (2017). Reducing intergroup bias through intergroup contact: Twenty years of progress and future directions. *Group Processes & Intergroup Relations, 20*(5), 606–620. https://doi.org/10.1177/1368430217712052

Eagly, A. H., & Karau, S. J. (2002). Role congruity theory of prejudice toward female leaders. *Psychological Review, 109*(3), 573–598. http://doi.org/10.1037//0033-295X.109.3.573

Eagly, A. H., Nater, C., Miller, D. I., Kaufmann, M., & Sczesny, S. (2020). Gender stereotypes have changed: A cross-temporal meta-analysis of U.S. public opinion polls from 1946 to 2018. *American Psychologist, 75*(3), 301–315. https://doi.org/10.1037/amp0000494

Fiske, S. T., Cuddy, A. J., Glick, P., & Xu, J. (2002). A model of (often mixed) stereotype content: Competence and warmth respectively follow from perceived status and competition. *Journal of Personality and Social Psychology, 82*(6), 878–902. https://doi.org/10.1037/0022-3514.82.6.878

Fiske, S. T., & Taylor, S. E. (2013). *Social cognition: From brains to culture.* Sage

Freud, S. (1917). The Taboo of virginity. *Standard Edition*, London 1953: 11: 191:208

Frost, D. M. (2011). Social stigma and its consequences for the socially stigmatized. *Social and Personality Psychology Compass, 5*(11), 824–839. https://doi.org/10.1111/j.1751-9004.2011.00394.x

Glick, P., & Fiske, S. T. (1996). The ambivalent sexism inventory: Differentiating hostile and benevolent sexism. *Journal of Personality and Social Psychology, 70*(3), 491–512. https://doi.org/10.1037/0022-3514.70.3.491

Goffman, E. (1963). *Stigma: Notes on the management of spoiled identity.* Prentice Hall

Golombok, S., & Fivush, R. (1994). *Gender development.* Cambridge University Press

Gwin, P. (2014, April 5). *Revisiting the Rwandan Genocide: Hutu and Tutsi.* National Geograpic. https://www.nationalgeographic.com/photography/proof/2014/04/05/revisiting-the-rwandan-genocide-hutu-or-tutsi/

Hammond, M. D., Milojev, P., Huang, Y., & Sibley, C. G. (2018). Benevolent sexism and hostile sexism across the ages. *Social Psychological and Personality Science, 9*(7), 863–874. https://doi.org/10.1177/1948550617727588

Hertz-Tang, A., & Carnes, M. (2020). Gender Stereotypes. In C. M. Stonnington & J. A. Files. *Burnout in women physicians: Prevention, treatment, and management* (pp. 79–103). Springer

Hess, T. M., & Hinson, J. T. (2006). Age-related variation in the influences of aging stereotypes on memory in adulthood. *Psychology and Aging, 21*(3), 621. https://doi.org/10.1037/0882-7974.21.3.621

Hofmann, W., Gawronski, B., Gschwendner, T., Le, H., & Schmitt, M. (2005). A meta-analysis on the correlation between the Implicit Association Test and explicit self-report measures. *Personality and Social Psychology Bulletin, 31*(10), 1369–1385. https://doi.org/10.1177/0146167205275613

Holroyd, J., Scaife, R., & Stafford, T. (2017). Responsibility for implicit bias. *Philosophy Compass, 12*(3), e12420. http://doi.org/10.1111/phc3.12410

Hutchings, P. B., & Sullivan, K. E. (2019). Prejudice and the Brexit vote: A tangled web. *Palgrave Communications, 5*(1), 1–5. https://doi.org/10.1057/s41599-018-0214-5

Jetten, J., Mols, F., Healy, N., & Spears, R. (2017). "Fear of falling": Economic instability enhances collective angst among societies' wealthy class. *Journal of Social Issues, 73*(1), 61–79. https://doi.org/10.1111/josi.12204

Jones, J., & Mosher, W. D. (2013). Fathers' involvement with their children: United States, 2006–2010. *National health statistics reports;* no 71. National Center for Health Statistics.

Kaiser, C. R., & Wilkins, C. L. (2010). Group identification and prejudice: Theoretical and empirical advances and implications. *Journal of Social Issues, 66*(3), 461–476. https://doi.org/10.1111/j.1540-4560.2010.01656.x

Konrad, A. M., Kramer, V., & Erkut, S. (2008). Critical mass: The impact of three or more women on corporate boards. *Organizational Dynamics, 37*(2), 145–164. https://doi.org/10.1016/j.orgdyn.2008.02.005

Lai, C. K., Hoffman, K. M., & Nosek, B. A. (2013). Reducing implicit prejudice. *Social and Personality Psychology Compass, 7*(5), 315–330. https://doi.org/10.1111/spc3.12023

LaPiere, R. T., & Farnsworth, P. R. (1949). *Social psychology* (3rd ed.). McGraw-Hill

Lemmer, G., & Wagner, U. (2015). Can we really reduce ethnic prejudice outside the lab? A meta-analysis of direct and indirect contact interventions. *European Journal of Social Psychology, 45*(2), 152–168. https://doi.org/10.1002/ejsp.2079

Lewis, Jr, N. A., & Sekaquaptewa, D. (2016). Beyond test performance: A broader view of stereotype threat. *Current Opinion in Psychology, 11*, 40–43. https://doi.org/10.1016/j.copsyc.2016.05.002

Madon, S., Guyll, M., Aboufadel, K., Montiel, E., Smith, A., Palumbo, P., & Jussim, L. (2001). Ethnic and national stereotypes: The Princeton trilogy revisited and revised. *Personality and Social Psychology Bulletin, 27*(8), 996–1010. https://doi.org/10.1177/0146167201278007

Major, B., & O'brien, L. T. (2005). The social psychology of stigma. *Annual Review of. Psychology, 56*, 393–421. https://doi.org/10.1146/annurev. psych.56.091103.070137

Meeussen, L., Van Laar, C., & Van Grootel, S. (2020). How to foster male engagement in traditionally female communal roles and occupations: Insights from research on gender norms and precarious manhood. *Social Issues and Policy Review, 14*(1), 297–328. https://doi.org/10.1111/sipr.12060

Meeussen, L., Veldman, J., & Van Laar, C. (2016). Combining gender, work, and family identities: The cross-over and spill-over of gender norms into young adults' work and family aspirations. *Frontiers in Psychology, 7*, 1–11. https://doi.org/10.3389/fpsyg.2016.01781.

Miller, C. T., Rothblum, E. D., Felicio, D., & Brand, P. (1995). Compensating for stigma: Obese and nonobese women's reactions to being visible. *Personality and Social Psychology Bulletin, 21*(10), 1093–1106. https://doi.org/10.1177/01461672952110010

Molina, L. E., Tropp, L. R., & Goode, C. (2016). Reflections on prejudice and intergroup relations. *Current Opinion in Psychology, 11*, 120–124. https://doi.org/10.1016/j.copsyc.2016.08.001

Murphy, M. C., Steele, C. M., & Gross, J. J. (2007). Signaling threat: How situational cues affect women in math, science, and engineering settings. *Psychological Science, 18*(10), 879–885. https://doi.org/10.1111/j.1467-9280.2007.01995.x

Nagle, J., & Clancy, M. A. C. (2010). *Shared society or benign Apartheid?: Understanding peace-building in divided societies.* Palgrave Macmillan

Newheiser, A. K., & Barreto, M. (2014). Hidden costs of hiding stigma: Ironic interpersonal consequences of concealing a stigmatized identity in social interactions. *Journal of Experimental Social Psychology, 52*, 58–70. https://doi.org/10.1016/j.jesp.2014.01.002

Onyeador, I. N., Wittlin, N. M., Burke, S. E., Dovidio, J. F., Perry, S. P., Hardeman, R. R., … van Ryn, M. (2020). The value of interracial contact for reducing anti-black bias among non-black physicians: A cognitive habits and growth evaluation (CHANGE) study report. *Psychological Science, 31*(1), 18–30. https://doi.org/10.1177/0956797619879139

Paterson, J. L., Brown, R., & Walters, M. A. (2019). The short and longer term impacts of hate crimes experienced directly, indirectly, and through the media. *Personality and Social Psychology Bulletin, 45*(7), 994–1010. https://doi.org/10.1177/0146167218802835

Payne, B. K., Vuletich, H. A., & Brown-Iannuzzi, J. L. (2019). Historical roots of implicit bias in slavery. *Proceedings of the National Academy of Sciences, 116*(24), 11693–11698. https://doi.org/10.1073/pnas.1818816116

Payscale. (2020, March). *The state of the gender pay gap in 2020.* https://www.payscale.com/data/gender-pay-gap#section03

Pettigrew, T. F., & Tropp, L. R. (2006). A meta-analytic test of intergroup contact theory. *Journal of Personality and Social Psychology, 90*(5), 751–783. https://doi.org/10.1037/0022-3514.90.5.751

Scheepers, D., Ellemers, N., & Sintemaartensdijk, N. (2009). Suffering from the possibility of status loss: Physiological responses to social identity threat in high status groups. *European Journal of Social Psychology, 39*(6), 1075–1092. https://doi.org/10.1002/ejsp.609

Scheepers, D., Spears, R., Doosje, B., & Manstead, A. S. R. (2006). Diversity in in-group bias: Structural factors, situational features, and social functions. *Journal of Personality and Social Psychology, 90*(6), 944–960. https://doi.org/10.1037/0022-3514.90.6.944

Schmitt, M. T., Branscombe, N. R., Kobrynowicz, D., & Owen, S. (2002). Perceiving discrimination against one's gender group has different implications for well-being in women and men. *Personality and Social Psychology Bulletin, 28*(2), 197–210. https://doi.org/10.1177/0146167202282006

Sczesny, S., Nater, C., & Eagly, A. H. (2019). Agency and communion: Their implications for gender stereotypes and gender identities. In A. Abele & B. Wojciszke (Eds.), *Agency and communion in social psychology* (pp. 103–116). Routledge

Spencer, S. J., Steele, C. M., & Quinn, D. M. (1999). Stereotype threat and women's math performance. *Journal of Experimental Social Psychology, 35*(1), 4–28. https://doi.org/10.1006/jesp.1998.1373

Steele, C. M., & Aronson, J. (1995). Stereotype threat and the intellectual test performance of African Americans. *Journal of Personality and Social Psychology, 69*(5), 797–811. https://doi.org/10.1037/0022-3514.69.5.797

Stone, J. (2002). Battling doubt by avoiding practice: The effects of stereotype threat on self-handicapping in white athletes. *Personality and Social Psychology Bulletin, 28*(12), 1667–1678.

Tajfel, H., Billig, M. G., Bundy, R. P., & Flament, C. (1971). Social categorization and intergroup behaviour. *European Journal of Social Psychology, 1*(2), 149–178. https://doi.org/10.1002/ejsp.2420010202

Tajfel, H., & Turner, J. C. (1979). An integrative theory of intergroup conflict. In W. G. Austin & S. Worchel (Eds.), *The social psychology of intergroup relations* (pp. 33–48). Brooks/Cole.

Tropp, L. R., & Pettigrew, T. F. (2005). Relationships between intergroup contact and prejudice among minority and majority status groups. *Psychological Science, 16*(12), 951–957. https://doi.org/10.1111/j.1467-9280.2005.01643.x

Wilde, A., & Diekman, A. B. (2005). Cross-cultural similarities and differences in dynamic stereotypes: A comparison between Germany and the United States. *Psychology of Women Quarterly, 29*(2), 188–196. https://doi.org/10.1111/j.1471-6402.2005.00181.x

6

THE SELF AS A COMMUNICATOR

In this book, we've covered how our self and our identity are influenced by others, often without us realising it. In Chapter 2, we discussed how our social world is an embedded part of our self, and as a result, we may not notice the impact it has on our attitudes and our beliefs. In Chapters 4 and 5, we went into depth about how we are influenced by groups of others and how the relationships that exist between groups shape who we are. Across these discussions, there has been one common theme: they all depend on communication. Indeed, no social process could exist without humans communicating with one another. For this reason, I have devoted an entire chapter to this topic.

Communication takes many forms; everything from our emails to our hair styles sends a message. Generally, we can classify communication into three main categories. *Visual communication* involves the transmission of ideas using symbols and imagery. Examples might include signs, graphics, and films. Few of us would deny the power that a picture can have on our feelings and beliefs (e.g., Box 3.2). *Non-verbal communication* consists of the behavioural elements of communication, such as facial expressions, body language, and posture. If you've ever had the experience of trying to hide your emotions only to have others guess exactly what you are thinking, you will know how difficult this form of communication is to control (DePaulo et al., 2003). One example of this can be found in a study of Olympic medal winners. The study showed that although all of the medal-winning athletes smiled on the podium, observers could accurately detect whether the athletes had genuine smiles or

DOI: 10.4324/9780429274534-6

'social smiles' (i.e., smiling for the sake of the camera; Matsumoto & Willingham, 2006). Interestingly, gold and bronze medal winners had more genuine smiles than silver medal winners; it seemed that those who came in second struggled to hide their disappointment at missing out on the top prize!

This chapter will focus on *verbal communication* or the production of spoken language that sends an intentional message to a listener. The emphasis will be on demonstrating the fundamental role language plays in shaping the way we perceive ourselves and others. We will discuss several ways that language can influence these perceptions – from how it shapes our relationship with those around us to its contribution to the inequalities between groups. To start, let's consider how our language influences key social identities.

LANGUAGE AS KEY TO IDENTITY

Some of our most important social identities rely on language. To illustrate this, let's consider someone who has immigrated from Mexico to the United States. Based on the level of attachment they feel toward each country, they might identify as Mexican, as American, and/or as Mexican American. Each of these identities is influenced by whether, and how well, they speak the dominant language in each country. For instance, their ability to speak Spanish might increase their identification with other Mexican- or Spanish-speaking immigrants. At the same time, how well they speak English will be an important factor in determining their engagement in their new culture and, by extension, how identified they are with their new country.

Researchers have acknowledged the importance of language in shaping our social identities. John J. Gumperz, one of the founders of Sociolinguistics, argued that "social identity and ethnicity are in large part established and maintained through language" (Gumperz & Cook-Gumperz, 1982), while early social identity theorists, Howard Giles and colleagues, developed frameworks to understand how this happens (see Gallois et al., 2005). One such framework is *ethnolinguistic identity theory* (ELIT; Giles & Johnson, 1987). One's *ethnolinguistic identity* is the feeling of belonging to a group that is based on a common ancestry and language (Noels, 2017). Just like any social identity, people are motivated to maintain the positive distinctiveness of this group. By applying social identity theory to one's ethnolinguistic identity, ELIT outlines the process in which this happens. It proposes that, just like any social identity, perceptions of permeability and legitimacy (or stability) determine whether members of a linguistic group engage in social mobility strategies, social creativity strategies, or collective action to feel good about their group (see Chapter 3).

To show how these strategies play out within the context of language, let's return to our previous example of a Mexican immigrant to the United States (let's call her Mia). Speaking Spanish in the United States is likely to mark her as an immigrant, a group that is generally low in power and often disliked by nationals (Havermans & Verkuyten, 2021). If Mia sees boundaries into the non-immigrant (i.e., the higher status group) as permeable, she may attempt to pass as a member of this group using social mobility strategies. These might include avoiding speaking Spanish or not teaching the language to her children (see Bilewicz et al., 2021). If boundaries seem impermeable and status relations legitimate, Mia might engage in social creativity strategies. This could take the form of comparing herself to a group she perceives as being more disadvantaged than her own (for instance, a smaller linguistic group with less speakers). Finally, if boundaries are impermeable but status differences feel illegitimate, then conditions may be rife for collective action. For Mia, this might involve campaigning for Spanish to be given equal status to English in the United States (Harwood & Vincze, 2012).

As with any social identity, achieving positive distinctiveness for one's ethnolinguistic identity depends on perceptions of group status. However, for language, status goes beyond whether speakers feel good about their group; it can determine whether a language will thrive, or even survive, in an intergroup context (Giles et al., 1977; Clément & Norton, 2021). ELIT proposes that for linguistic groups, status is expressed through *ethnolinguistic vitality*. This is made up of three key factors: *demographic vitality* (i.e., the number of speakers within a linguistic community), *institutional support* (i.e., support for the language's use in settings such as schools or government buildings), and *status vitality* (i.e., the level of prestige it holds; Bourhis et al., 2019). How a language fares on each of these dimensions influences whether the linguistic group is at risk of becoming endangered and disappearing altogether. If the number of language speakers dwindles (low demographic vitality), there is a lack of support for its use in key areas of society (low institutional support), and it is perceived as generally unimportant (low status vitality), then it is less likely that people will want to learn that language. In addition, those who do speak it may be less inclined to teach it to their children (Clément & Norton, 2021), further contributing to the threat of extinction.

BOX 6.1   APPLYING ETHNOLINGUISTIC VITALITY TO WELSH

To understand how ethnolinguistic vitality can be applied to the real world, let's look to Welsh. Although the language dates to 600 BC, the Tudor period brought policies that suppressed its use in public life (e.g., it was banned in schools, courts, workplaces, etc.). From the perspective of ELIT, these practices meant that the language began suffering from low institutional support. Discrimination against the Welsh language continued into the mid-20th century (Brain, n.d.) resulting in increasingly less people speaking it over time (i.e., low demographic vitality). These factors may have fed the general perception that Welsh, as a language, was dying (i.e., low-status vitality). By 2011, only 19% of the Welsh population reported that they were able to speak Welsh (Office of National Statistics, 2011). However, that same year, the *Welsh Language Measure* was introduced, an act that ensured the equal treatment of Welsh and English (thus cementing Welsh's status in society by increasing institutional vitality). Only 10 years later, the number of Welsh speakers in Wales had risen to 29.5%, marking a significant increase in demographic vitality (Welsh Government, 2021). Today, Welsh is the fastest growing language in the United Kingdom and no longer considered endangered by the United Nations Educational, Scientific and Cultural Organization (The National Reporter, 2022).

Given its influence on who we are, it seems clear that language goes beyond transmitting information from one person to another. Rather, it plays an integral role in shaping our self. However, it's not just which language we speak that influences who we are, but *how* we speak that language. Over the next three sections, we will discuss the ways in which our self and our identity are shaped by words: how we pronounce them and the ones we choose. To begin, we will be applying many of the concepts we've discussed so far in this book to one of the most powerful markers of group membership: our accent.

ACCENTS AS KEY TO IDENTITY

When we think about accents, we often think about the ways other people speak. However, an *accent,* defined as any speech pattern that is more or less similar to the standard within a population, is something that everyone has (Kinzler, 2021). In the United Kingdom, the standard accent is called *Received Pronunciation (RP) English* (aka the 'Queens English'; Levon et al., 2021). Other accents can be classified into three main groups: *regional* (e.g., Cockney accent), *foreign* (i.e., native English accents that are not British, such as an Australian accent), or *non-native* (i.e., the accent of any speaker who has not spoken English since birth). Importantly, all accents give clues to the speaker's ethnicity, social class, education, age, nationality, and region of birth (Dragojevic et al., 2021). Let's go back to our example of Mia, a Mexican immigrant to the United States. The strength of her accent when she speaks English could indicate how long she has been living in the United States. The way she speaks Spanish might reveal clues to the part of Mexico she is from. Importantly, one's accent intersects with their other social identities (see Chapter 2): When forming impressions of Mia, the information deduced from her speech patterns will contribute to the information deduced from her other category markers. For example, in some of my own work, we found that people considered a person's nationality as well as the strength of their accent when forming impressions. Indeed, after detecting even slight dissimilarities in a person's speech patterns, the first question we tend to ask is "Where are you from?" (Birney et al., 2020a).

The power of accents to shape perceptions of our self and others is profound. As an indicator of out-group membership, multiple studies have shown that one's accent is more meaningful than one's race (e.g., Pietraszewski & Schwartz, 2014). As an example, let's imagine a White British person who meets two people: one is of Asian descent but speaks like them, and the other is White but speaks with an Eastern European accent. According to the research in this area, the White British person is more likely to see the person of Asian descent as in-group and the other White person as out-group based on their speech patterns (Rakić et al., 2011). It seems that this penchant for similar speech patterns starts early: at 5 months old, babies show a preference for speakers with accents that are like those of the people they are normally around (Kinzler et al., 2007). This bias becomes increasingly meaningful as we grow. By the age of ten, children favour the same accented speakers (over the same race speakers) when distributing resources (Spence & Imuta, 2020). By adolescence, young people assume that a shared accent indicates friendship, rather than a shared race or gender (Arredondo & Gelman, 2019).

Many people are surprised to think of accent in this way. After all, our comparisons of how different linguistic groups speak are often done in light-hearted conversations (while comparing how different racial groups look probably would not be). But, when we consider our evolutionary history, it's perhaps not that surprising that accents take precedence over race in how we categorise others. According to Kurzban et al. (2001), when humans lived in bands of hunters and gatherers, they were unlikely to encounter anyone who looked different than themselves. Therefore, they would have relied on speech patterns to determine whether someone unfamiliar was a member of their own group or that of a potentially threatening out-group (Cosmides et al., 2003). Today, humans are excellent at detecting even slight differences in speech patterns (de Jong, 2018), possibly because this ability may have evolved over time.

While a preference for the accent of one's in-group does not automatically result in discrimination (Liberman et al., 2017), there is a wealth of research showing that people are regularly discriminated against based on how they speak. With everything else equal, people with non-standard accents are judged as less suitable for leadership positions, less effective educators, and more likely to be judged as having committed crimes compared to people with standard accents (Dragojevic et al., 2021). However, it's important to note that whether an accent is considered as standard depends on the social context. Let's take the example of a student from Yorkshire, England, who speaks with a Northern English accent. Because this way of speaking is in line with the standard in his community, he might not think much about it when he's in his home county.

However, if he goes to an academic conference and people's speech patterns are more in line with the British standard accent (i.e., RP English), he may become aware and even self-conscious about his Northern dialect. Just like any social identity, certain contexts can make our linguistic identity salient and, as such, guide our thinking and our behaviour (see Chapter 2).

One reason our student may feel uncomfortable about his accent in this new environment is that he is likely aware of the stigma attached to it (see Chapter 5). In the United Kingdom, speakers with accents that deviate from RP English are judged as less educated and lower in socio-economic status (Levon et al., 2021). Regional accents also tend to be rated as less 'correct' than standard accents (Hiraga, 2005). As our student is at an academic conference, an environment where intelligence is especially valued, he may be vulnerable to experiencing stereotype threat because of how he speaks (see Chapter 5). To manage this stigma, he might avoid interactions with others or attempt to imitate the accent of the speakers at the conference (Barreto, 2015). The former will make it more difficult to network and the latter is likely to backfire. Because it is very difficult for most people to change their accent, trying to sound like someone else can come across as disingenuous (Birney et al., 2020b). Regardless, the cognitive burdens that come with the management of accent stigma serve to entrench the disadvantage the student faces.

Despite the evidence that accent-based discrimination is rife (e.g., Levon et al., 2021), most laws offer little support for non-standard speakers. In the United States, employers who deem a candidate's accent to be unintelligible are protected from charges of discrimination. Yet, there is no way to assess this claim objectively. Considering that listeners are adept at adapting to unfamiliar speech patterns (Melguy & Johnson, 2021), it is prejudice that likely drives claims about the clarity of others' speech (Rubin, 1992). Furthermore, because other social identities such as race and ethnicity intersect with accent but are protected under the law, claims about a speaker's intelligibility could be used as a 'legitimate' way to discriminate against these characteristics (Gluszek & Dovidio, 2010). A 2008 study by the European Commission found that 45% of managers across 26 countries believed that having a non-standard accent is a disadvantage in the workplace. The prevalence (and openness) of such sentiments has led some scholars to identify accent discrimination as the "last acceptable form of prejudice" (Akomolafe, 2020). While efforts to eliminate practices that disadvantage non-standard speakers are increasing (e.g., France outlawed the discrimination of regional accents in 2020), accent remains a means of discrimination that, like any stigmatised identity, has implications for the speaker's sense of self (see Chapter 5).

In this section, we considered how language, by way of one's accent, is not only a social identity in and of itself but can guide perceptions about other social identities we have. We also considered how accents are discriminated against, often in a way that is generally protected to the point where it can be considered acceptable. Finally, we touched upon the repercussions that accent stigma can have on one's opportunities and their relationships with others. In the next section, we move on to how language impacts group-level dynamics. Although hearing an individual speaker's non-standard accent can impact perceptions of out-groups (Birney et al., 2020b), how we use language, through the words we choose, has been shown to play a subtle, yet crucial role in the way that stereotypes are formed and perpetuated. However, before discussing these processes, I will give an overview of how we use language to manage our interpersonal relationships and, by extension, the boundaries between groups.

LANGUAGE ACCOMMODATION

Imagine you are talking to your friend Sophie about a shared acquaintance called Mary. You are aware that Sophie and Mary are meeting for drinks, and you want Sophie to know that Mary tends to avoid spending money. To convey this message about Mary, you have several adjectives available to you. Some have negative connotations (e.g., stingy, cheap, tight), while others are more positive (e.g., thrifty, prudent, careful). Which word will you choose? According to Higgins and Rholes (1978), your choice will depend on how you think Sophie feels about Mary. If you believe Sophie likes Mary, you will be more likely to describe her using a more positive word, such as thrifty. If you think Sophie dislikes Mary, you will likely use a negative word, such as stingy.

or emphasise their higher status. To do this, the professor may accentuate differences between how they communicate and how their student communicates (e.g., by speaking formally or requesting that the student use titles).

In addition to shaping interpersonal relationships, the way we accommodate our language can shape the relationship between groups. As in the example above, the professor manages their relationship by using language to either bond with or to distance themselves from their student. For both parties, this experience might influence future interactions, shaping the relationship between students and professors more generally. Even on a national level, how language is accommodated helps to enhance in-group solidarity and exclude out-groups (see Box 6.2). For example, in Taiwan, the shift to speaking the Taiwanese dialect, Southern Min, over Mandarin Chinese in the 1990s was one way to distinguish their identity from that of China (Chuang, 2004). Other examples of how language helps to form and maintain group identities can be found in the dialects of minority groups. For instance, African American Vernacular English (or, AAVE) serves to maintain Black American's distinctiveness from other groups (Filmer, 2003). Hence, in addition to easing the communication process and influencing interpersonal relations, language accommodation is a tool that both creates and maintains group boundaries.

In this section, we reviewed how we alter our language depending on factors such as the beliefs of our communication partner and our goals for the exchange. We also covered the consequence of language accommodation for our own thoughts and beliefs, as well as the repercussions it has for interpersonal perceptions and by extension, the dynamic between groups. In the next section, we discuss the link between language and intergroup relations further, focusing specifically on how the words we use can perpetuation group stereotypes.

BOX 6.2 LANGUAGE AS NATIONAL IDENTITY – BRITISH ENGLISH VS. AMERICAN ENGLISH

In the 1887 story, *The Canterville Ghost*, Oscar Wilde famously stated "we have really everything in common with America nowadays, except, of course, language." Over 135 years later, the statement can still get a chuckle from English speakers on both sides of the Atlantic. This is because differences in pronunciation, grammar, and spelling continue to distinguish British English from American English. For instance, when spelling common words, the preference in American English is to omit the letter "u" (e.g., color vs. colour) and to use "z" instead of "s" (e.g., realize vs realise). Grammar is different as well: British English would describe Joe as *in* hospital, while American English would see Joe as *in the* hospital. There are also many examples of entirely different words used to describe the same thing (e.g., pacifier vs. dummy, trunk vs. boot, sneakers vs. trainers).

Why is this? And how have these differences endured despite the rise of globalisation over the last century? One answer relies on the way language has been used to reflect and maintain each country's individual identity. Before 1600, English was spoken only in Britain. However, as the British expanded their empire over the next 150 years, they spread their language around the world. Over time, British settlements began forming their own identities and, as part of this, started adapting the language. By the time the American colonies declared their independence from Britain in 1776, they had formed their own version of English. In line with the idea that language is key to a group's identity, this new version of English became a source of pride for the new nation: it not only reflected their independence from Britain but constantly reinforced their new American identity (Strevens, 1992). In fact, support for American nationalism and cultural independence was a primary motivator for author Noah Webster's work in transforming the English language through his influential dictionaries (Kendall, 2010).

LANGUAGE AS KEY TO INTERGROUP RELATIONS

For the 2014 Christmas season, a popular UK retail chain released a greeting card that was meant to be funny. The following sentence was on the card's front: "10 reasons why Santa Claus must live on a council estate." On the inside, the reasons listed included "He only works once per year" and "He wears the same, out-of-fashion clothes every day and never washes them." Although the card was withdrawn and an apology issued (Iqbal, 2014), this example highlights important questions about the role language plays in shaping our perceptions of groups.

According to Allport (1954), an important mechanism in which prejudiced ideas are formed and perpetuated is through language. After all, it is through words that we label categories we feel are socially significant (for instance, using 'he' and 'she' or labelling someone as 'young' or 'old'). The stereotypes that are associated with these labels are then culturally shared through communication. Because successful communication depends on a shared reality (Higgins et al., 2021), drawing on commonly known ideas about groups helps us get our message across. Unfortunately, this process also perpetuates incorrect notions about groups. To illustrate how this happens, let's use the following example: When describing his friend Tom to a colleague, Conor says 'Even though Tom is gay, he is quite manly.' This statement gives the colleague an understanding of what Tom is like based on culturally shared stereotypes about gay men being feminine. Through this exchange, Conor has perpetuated this stereotype, which acts to further embed this idea for his colleague. It is due to the ability of language to create and then cement ideas about groups that Allport (1954) so aptly described words as cutting 'slices through the human race.'

As problematic as the transmission of stereotypes is, it is unlikely that Conor meant any harm by his statement about Tom. In fact, he may consider Tom a friend and never think of himself as someone who would promote false and problematic narratives about his friend's social identity. Similarly, the colleague may not have thought much about the statement, except to feel that they have a better understanding of what Tom is like. Consider other common phrases such as 'Sarah is such a tomboy' or 'Alex throws like a girl.' Most of us will hear comments like these and not think to be offended by them. Yet, when you stop to consider them more carefully, the description of Sarah suggests that she is acting in a way that deviates from expectations associated with her gender. The statement about Alex's throwing ability is a well-known insult based on the idea that girls are weak and incompetent in sport. Most of us are rightfully uncomfortable with these types of blanket assumptions yet are unthinking or even accepting when we say or hear the very statements that make them.

According to Bruckmüller and Abele (2010), we tend to describe what we consider to deviate from what is normal. For example, you may hear someone allude to the 'male nurse' who cared for them in hospital, but it's unlikely you'd hear anyone refer to the nurse who took their blood as a 'female nurse.' Rather, the latter is usually called a 'nurse.' Because we assume that nurses are female, we feel the need to describe the difference we see when we come across someone who does not fit this stereotype (i.e., the nurse who is male). Not only does this tendency perpetuate ideas about what is normal and what is not, but also research shows that we make further inferences about the groups that we explain. For instance, in contexts where one group is assumed to be the norm (e.g., men in leadership positions), we tend to use them as the default group when we describe groups that we consider to be less normative (e.g., women in leadership positions). Hence, when talking about people in leadership roles, we compare women to men, rather than men to women (e.g., 'women's leadership styles tend to be different than men's leadership styles' rather than 'men's leadership styles tend to be different than women's'; Bruckmüller & Braun, 2020). The consequences of this are surprisingly far-reaching: not only do people tend to rely more heavily on stereotypes when statements are based on societal notions of what is normal, but they also perceived the status differences between groups to be both larger and more legitimate (Bruckmüller et al., 2012).

In addition to the order in which we compare groups, the way we use nouns and adjectives can amplify stereotypes. Nouns categorise people by assigning them to specific groups (e.g., Sarah is an intellectual), while adjectives are used to describe one of (usually) many qualities that a person might possess (e.g., Sarah is intellectual). Researchers have found that describing people using nouns elicits more stereotypical inferences about a person than when describing them using adjectives. For instance, describing Mark as *a* homosexual (noun) rather than *as* homosexual (adjective) resulted in assumptions that not only would Mark act in line with stereotypical assumptions that tend to be associated with gay men, but he is also unlikely to act in ways that counter these stereotypes (Carnaghi et al., 2008).

The role that language plays in perpetuating ideas about groups is subtle and may feel impossible to change. After all, it is difficult to break ingrained habits, especially with something like sentence construction which, for most of us, feels automatic. But once we become aware of how language maintains problematic ideas about groups, it becomes easier to recognise its presence in our own and in other's communication. If we are ever unsure of whether a statement promotes harmful ideas about groups, a good tip is to replace the group we are describing with another group. To illustrate how this works, let's go back to the example of the card about Santa living on a council estate. If we replace 'council estate' with 'Black people,' it will likely become clear that neither sentence is appropriate: a card evidencing supposed reasons that Santa is Black because he 'only works on day a year' doesn't feel funny or, even, okay to say. Logically, if it's not okay to make this joke about one group, then it's not okay to make the joke about another group.

Once we recognise when language is promoting harmful ideas about groups, we can work to correct it. Bruckmüller and Braun (2020) give some useful advice on how to do this. In their research, they point out that when talking about gender inequalities in the workplace, we tend to focus on women's disadvantage, rather than men's advantage. The researchers explain that most of us will have heard that women are under-represented in leadership positions and paid less than their male counterparts. What we don't often hear is the problem framed in the reverse: that men tend to be *over*-represented in leadership positions and *over*paid compared to their female counterparts. Bruckmüller and Braun (2020) showed that the former framing is problematic for tackling this inequality; upon hearing how women are under-represented, people tended to consider solutions aimed at helping women rather than solutions that would tackle the systematic inequalities that contribute to gender inequalities. However, they do not believe that the answer lies in the latter framing. First, being reminded of privilege can feel threatening to advantaged groups (in this example, men in leadership positions). Second, people tend to pay more attention to information that feels negative (e.g., women's disadvantage) rather than information that feels positive (e.g., men's advantage). Instead, they recommend framing the issue more evenly, for instance, by mentioning women's disadvantage as well as men's advantage. It is okay to state that women are under-represented in leadership but, to avoid the interpretation that this is an issue that is only relevant to women, the communicator should also highlight the structural barriers that women face (Bruckmüller & Braun, 2020).

By building an awareness of how we use language, we can make a difference in promoting a fairer world. The good news is that we are getting better at recognising the contribution language makes to inequality. For instance, within the medical profession, there has been a shift from calling people by their disease (e.g., a diabetic) towards a description that is less defining (e.g., a person with diabetes; Helgeson & Zajdel, 2017). In education, there has been a call to rethink the use of labels (e.g., LDs for learning disabilities) after it was found that part of the achievement gap between labelled and non-labelled students could be attributed to the stigma attached to the label rather than the condition itself (Shifrer, 2013). Even the media has jumped on the bandwagon. To acknowledge its role in perpetuating group stereotypes, Disney added content warnings before many of their classic films warning of the 'negative depictions and/or mistreatment of...cultures' (BBC, 2020). While we still have a way to go in understanding and addressing the harm that our words can have, we can all play a part by reflecting on our own language and that of those around us.

CONCLUSION

We started this chapter by making the argument that communication is at the heart of all social processes; none of the concepts covered in this book could exist without it. To make this point, we have applied many of the processes discussed in this book to communication and to our use of language generally: language allows us to create a shared sense of reality with others, which helps fulfil some of our most basic psychological needs (Chapter 2). Theories such as ELIT and CAT explain how language helps us manage our various social identities depending on the context we are in and our perception of others (Chapter 3). The effect that language accommodation, whether through audience tuning or divergence, has on our attitudes, beliefs, and thoughts makes it a powerful social influence (Chapter 4). Finally, language-based stigma and the way that our use of language can perpetuate stereotypes serve to entrench inequalities between groups (Chapter 5).

Yet, while this chapter makes clear how language ties to other social processes, it is important to remember that communication is a process in and of itself. For instance, although our linguistic group intersects with other social identities, it also constitutes an important identity on its own. Even though perceptions associated with non-standard accents can result in the discrimination of other identities, stigma that is based specifically on one's language has its own implications for the speaker. And, while there are many factors that influence the relationship between groups, our way of using language is a key force for perpetuating stereotypes. Hence, when considering our self and our identity, the impact of language, and of communication more generally, cannot be overstated.

CHAPTER SUMMARY

- The language we speak intersects with other social identities (e.g., our ethnicity, nationality, etc.) while also serving as a key identity in and of itself.
- Accommodating our language (either towards or away from our communication partner) helps us manage our interpersonal relationships and the boundaries between groups.
- How we speak, by way of our accent, influences how we are perceived and can serve as a basis for prejudice and discrimination.
- The words we use can entrench stereotypes and can shape intergroup relations.

WANT TO KNOW MORE?

Recommended Reading:
- Gasiorek, J., & Aune, R. K. (2021). *Creating understanding: How communicating aligns minds*. Peter Lang
- Giles, H. (2016). *Communication accommodation theory: Negotiating personal relationships and social identities across contexts*. Cambridge University Press
- Kinzler, K. D. (2020). *How you say it: Why we judge others by the way they talk and the costs of this hidden bias*. Houghton Mifflin Harcourt

REFERENCES

Akomolafe, O. (2020). African-born scholars and accent discrimination: The last acceptable form of prejudice. In *African Scholars and intellectuals in North American academies* (pp. 199–226). Routledge

Allport, G. W. (1954). *The nature of prejudice.* Addison-Wesley

Arredondo, M. M., & Gelman, S. A. (2019). Do varieties of Spanish influence US Spanish–English bilingual children's friendship judgments? *Child Development, 90*(2), 655–671. https://doi.org/10.1111/cdev.12932

Barreto, M. (2015). Experiencing and coping with social stigma. In M. Mikulincer, P. R. Shaver, J. F. Dovidio, & J. A. Simpson (Eds.) *APA handbook of personality and social psychology, Volume 2: Group processes* (pp. 473–506).

BBC. (2020, October 16) *Disney updates content warning for racism in classic films.* https://www.bbc.co.uk/news/world-us-canada-54566087

Bilewicz, M., Skrodzka, M., Olko, J., & Lewińska, T. (2021). The double-edged sword of identification. The divergent effects of identification on acculturation stress among Ukrainian immigrants in Poland. *International Journal of Intercultural Relations, 83,* 177–186. https://doi.org/10.1016/j.ijintrel.2021.06.009

Birney, M. E., Rabinovich, A., & Morton, T. A. (2020a). Where are you from? An investigation into the intersectionality of accent strength and nationality status on perceptions of non-native speakers in Britain. *Journal of Language and Social Psychology, 39*(4), https://doi.org/10.1177/0261927X20933315

Birney, M. E., Rabinovich, A., Morton, T. A., Heath, H. & Ashcroft, S. (2020b). When speaking English is not enough: The consequences of language-based stigma for non-native speakers. *Journal of Language and Social Psychology, 39*(1), 67–86. http://doi.org/10.1177/0261927X19883906

Bourhis, R. Y., Sachdev, I., Ehala, M., & Giles, H. (2019). Assessing 40 years of group vitality research and future directions. *Journal of Language and Social Psychology, 38*(4), 409–422. https://doi.org/10.1177/0261927X19868974

Brain, J. (n.d.). The Welsh Language. *Historic UK.* https://www.historic-uk.com/HistoryUK/HistoryofWales/Welsh-Language/

Bruckmüller, S., & Abele, A. E. (2010). Comparison focus in intergroup comparisons: Who we compare to whom influences who we see as powerful and agentic. *Personality and Social Psychology Bulletin, 36*(10), 1424–1435

Bruckmüller, S., & Braun, M. (2020). One group's advantage or another group's disadvantage? How comparative framing shapes explanations of, and reactions to, workplace gender inequality. *Journal of Language and Social Psychology, 39*(4), 457–475

Bruckmüller, S., Hegarty, P., & Abele, A. E. (2012). Framing gender differences: Linguistic normativity affects perceptions of power and gender stereotypes. *European Journal of Social Psychology, 42*(2), 210–218. https://doi.org/10.1002/ejsp.858

Carnaghi, A., Maass, A., Gresta, S., Bianchi, M., Cadinu, M., & Arcuri, L. (2008). Nomina sunt omina: on the inductive potential of nouns and adjectives in person perception. *Journal of Personality and Social Psychology, 94*(5), 839

Chuang, R. (2004). *Theoretical perspectives: Fluidity and complexity of cultural and ethnic identity* (Vol. 65). Rowman and Littlefield

Clément, R., & Norton, B. (2021). Ethnolinguistic vitality, identity and power: Investment in SLA. *Journal of Language and Social Psychology, 40*(1), 154–171. https://doi.org/10.1177/0261927X20966734

Cosmides, L., Tooby, J., & Kurzban, R. (2003). Perceptions of race. *Trends in Cognitive Sciences, 7*(4), 173–179. https://doi.org/10.1016/S1364-6613(03)00057-3

De Jong, K. J. (2018). Sensitivity to foreign accent. *Acoust Today, 14,* 9–16

DePaulo, B. M., Lindsay, J. J., Malone, B. E., Muhlenbruck, L., Charlton, K., & Cooper, H. (2003). Cues to deception. *Psychological Bulletin, 129*(1), 74. https://doi.org/10.1037/0033-2909.129.1.74

Dragojevic, M., Fasoli, F., Cramer, J., & Rakić, T. (2021). Toward a century of language attitudes research: Looking back and moving forward. *Journal of Language and Social Psychology, 40*(1), 60–79. https://doi.org/10.1177/0261927X20966714

Echterhoff, G., & Higgins, E. T. (2018). Shared reality: Construct and mechanisms. *Current Opinion in Psychology, 23.* https://doi.org/10.1016/j.copsyc.2018.09.003

Echterhoff, G., Higgins, E. T., Kopietz, R., & Groll, S. (2008). How communication goals determine when audience tuning biases memory. *Journal of Experimental Psychology, 137*(1), 3–31. http://doi.org/10.1037/0096-3445.137.1.3

European Commission. (2008). *Discrimination in the European Union: Perceptions, experiences and attitudes.* https://health.ec.europa.eu/publications/discrimination-european-union-perceptions-experiences-and-attitudes_en

Filmer, A. A. (2003). African-American vernacular English: Ethics, ideology, and pedagogy in the conflict between identity and power. *World Englishes, 22*(3), 253–270

Gallois, C., Ogay, T., & Giles, H. (2005). Communication accommodation theory: A look back and a look ahead. In W. B. Gudykunst (Ed.). *Theorizing about intercultural communication* (pp. 121–148). Sage

Giles, H. (Ed.). (2016). *Communication accommodation theory: Negotiating personal relationships and social identities across contexts.* Cambridge University Press

Giles, H., Bourhis, R., & Taylor, D. M. (1977). Towards a theory of language in ethnic group relations. In H. Giles (Ed.), *Language, ethnicity and intergroup relations* (pp. 307–348). Academic Press

Giles, H., & Johnson, P. (1987). Ethnolinguistic identity theory: A social psychological approach to language maintenance. *International Journal of the Sociology of Language, 68,* 69–99. https://doi.org/10.1515/ijsl.1987.68.69

Gluszek, A., & Dovidio, J. F. (2010). The way they speak: A social psychological perspective on the stigma of nonnative accents in communication. *Personality and Social Psychology Review, 14*(2), 214–237. http://doi.org/10.1177/1088868309359288

Gregory, S. W., & Webster, S. (1996). A nonverbal signal in voices of interview partners effectively predicts communication accommodation and social status perceptions. *Journal of Personality and Social Psychology, 70*(6), 1231–1240. http://doi.org/10.1037/0022-3514.70.6.1231

Gumperz, J. J., & Cook-Gumperz, J. (1982). Introduction: Language and the communication of social identity. In J. J. Gumperz (Ed.), *Language and social identity* (pp. 1–22). Cambridge University Press

Harwood, J., & Vincze, L. (2012). Ethnolinguistic identity and television use in a minority language setting. *Journal of Media Psychology: Theories, Methods, and Applications, 24*(4), 135. https://doi.org/10.1027/1864-1105/a000071

Havermans, W., & Verkuyten, M. (2021). Positive and negative behavioural intentions towards immigrants: A question of ethnic categorisation or worldview conflict? *International Journal of Psychology, 56*(5), 633–641. https://doi.org/10.1002/ijop.12748

Helgeson, V. S., & Zajdel, M. (2017). Adjusting to chronic health conditions. *Annual Review of Psychology, 68*(1), 545–571. http://doi.org /10.1146/annurev-psych-010416–044014

Higgins, E. T. (1981). The "communication game:" Implications for social cognition and persuasion. In E. T. Higgins, C. P. Herman, & M. P. Zanna (Eds.), *Social cognition: The Ontario symposium* (Vol. 1, pp. 343–392). Erlbaum

Higgins, E. T. (1992). Achieving 'shared reality' in the communication game: A social action that create; meaning. *Journal of Language and Social Psychology, 11*(3), 107–131. https://doi.org/10.1177/0261927X92113001

Higgins, E. T., & Rholes, W. S. (1978). "Saying is believing": Effects of message modification on memory and liking for the person described. *Journal of Experimental Social Psychology, 14*, 363–378. https://doi.org/10.1016/0022-1031(78)90032-X

Higgins, E. T., Rossignac-Milon, M., & Echterhoff, G. (2021). Shared reality: From sharing-is-believing to merging minds. *Current Directions in Psychological Science, 30*(2), 103–110. https://doi.org/10.1177/0963721421992027

Hiraga, Y. (2005). British attitudes towards six varieties of English in the USA and Britain. *World Englishes, 24*(3), 289–308. https://doi.org/10.1111/j.0883-2919.2005.00411.x

Iqbal, N. (2014, December 7). Clinton Cards apologises over council estate card. *BBC*. https://www.bbc.co.uk/news/newsbeat-30368218

Kendall, J. (2010). *The forgotten founding father: Noah Webster's obsession and the creation of an American culture.* Penguin Group

Kinzler, K. D. (2021). Language as a social cue. *Annual Review of Psychology, 72*, 241–264. https://doi.org/10.1146/annurev-psych-010418-103034

Kinzler, K. D., Dupoux, E., & Spelke, E. S. (2007). The native language of social cognition. *The Proceedings of the National Academy of Sciences of the United States of America, 104*, 12577–12580. https://doi.org/10.1073/pnas.0705345104

Kurzban, R., Tooby, J., & Cosmides, L. (2001). Can race be erased? Coalitional computation and social categorization. *Proceedings of the National Academy of Sciences, 98*(26), 15387–15392. https://doi.org/10.1073/pnas.25154149

Levon, E., Sharma, D., Watt, D. J., Cardoso, A., & Ye, Y. (2021). Accent bias and perceptions of Professional competence in England. *Journal of English Linguistics, 49*(4), 355–388 https://doi.org/10.1177/00754242211046316

Liberman, Z., Woodward, A. L., & Kinzler, K. D. (2017). The origins of social categorization. *Trends in Cognitive Sciences, 21*(7), 556–568. https://doi.org/10.1016/j.tics.2017.04.004

Matsumoto, D., & Willingham, B. (2006). The thrill of victory and the agony of defeat: Spontaneous expressions of medal winners of the 2004 Athens Olympic games. *Journal of Personality and Social Psychology, 91*(3), 568–581. https://doi.org/10.1037/0022-3514.91.3.568

Melguy, Y. V., & Johnson, K. (2021). General adaptation to accented English: Speech intelligibility unaffected by perceived source of non-native accent. *The Journal of the Acoustical Society of America, 149*(4), 2602–2614. https://doi.org/10.1121/10.0004240

Noels, K. A. (2017). Identity, ethnolinguistic. *The International Encyclopedia of Intercultural Communication*, 1–10. https://doi.org/10.1002/9781118783665.ieicc0160

Office of National Statistics. (2011). *Language in England and Wales*. https://www.ons.gov.uk/peoplepopulationandcommunity/culturalidentity/language/articles/languageinenglandandwales/2013-03-04#welsh-language

Pietraszewski, D., & Schwartz, A. (2014). Evidence that accent is a dedicated dimension of social categorization, not a byproduct of coalitional categorization. *Evolution and Human Behavior, 35*(1), 51–57. https://doi.org/10.1016/j.evolhumbehav.2013.09.005

Pinelli, F., Davachi, L., & Higgins, E. T. (2022). Shared reality effects of tuning messages to multiple audiences. *Social Cognition, 40*(2), 172–183

Rakić, T., Steffens, M. C., & Mummendey, A. (2011). Blinded by the accent! The minor role of looks in ethnic categorization. *Journal of Personality and Social Psychology, 100*(1), 16. https://doi.org/10.1037/a0021522

Rubin, D. L. (1992). Nonlanguage factors affecting undergraduates' judgments of nonnative English-speaking teaching assistants. *Research in Higher Education, 33*(4), 511–531. https://doi.org/0.1007/BF00973770

Shifrer, D. (2013). Stigma of a label: Educational expectations for high school students labeled with learning disabilities. *Journal of Health and Social Behavior, 54*(4), 462–480. https://doi.org/10.1177/0022146513503346

Spence, J. L., & Imuta, K. (2020). Age-related changes in children's accent-based resource distribution. *Journal of Experimental Child Psychology, 193*, 104807. https://doi.org/10.1016/j.jecp.2020.104807

Strevens, P. (1992). English as an international language: Directions in the 1990s. In B. B. Kachru (Ed.), *The other tongue: English across cultures* (pp. 27–47). University of Illinois Press

The National Reporter. (2022, January 29). Welsh language not available on world's top 50 apps. *South Wales Argus.* https://www.southwalesargus.co.uk/news/19884104.welsh-language-not-available-worlds-top-50-apps/

Welsh Government. (2021). *Welsh language data from annual population survey: 2021.* https://gov.wales/welsh-language-data-annual-population-survey-2021

7

THE SELF AND SOCIETY

In this book, we've considered the self as a function of one's social identity. The first three chapters laid the groundwork for this thinking. In Chapter 1, we reviewed the ideas on selfhood from Western philosophy and psychology, helping set out the context in which current theorising on the self has developed. In Chapter 2, we summarised the evidence, suggesting that the self is formed through a person's group membership. In Chapter 3, we detailed how two theories – the social identity approach and intersectionality – explain selfhood. The next three chapters moved towards applying these ideas to real-world examples of human behaviour. In Chapter 4, we considered how the group a person is a part of influences their willingness to conform to and obey others, to support or resist tyranny, and to help those in need. In Chapter 5, we examined how the way that groups relate to each other influences the self, by zeroing in on how stereotypes, prejudice, and discrimination of people based on their group memberships affect both the targets and the perpetrators of these perceptions and actions. Finally, in Chapter 6, we explored the way that human communication, specifically language, shapes and reinforces both individual's social identities and the power dynamics that exist within and between groups.

One way we can apply the ideas discussed in these chapters is to consider how they relate to current structures in society, for instance, education, healthcare, and places of work. However, addressing these contexts in any depth would require a whole other book (or likely, three!). Therefore, this final chapter will address one area that all these contexts have in common, but where identity

DOI: 10.4324/9780429274534-7

is a determinant of its success: their organizational structure. Within organizations, the social identity approach has added to our understanding of how to foster success within areas such as motivation, commitment, decision-making, productivity, conflict, and stress (Haslam, 2004). In this final chapter, we will concentrate on one area that underlies all of these: leadership. Leadership – both bad and good, and both effective and ineffective – influences all these processes, playing a key role in how organizations function. Drawing from the book, *The New Psychology of Leadership* by S. Alexander Haslam, Stephen D. Reicher, and Michael Platow (2020), we will consider leadership from a social identity perspective.

A SOCIAL IDENTITY APPROACH TO LEADERSHIP

Around 380 BC, Plato described leaders as 'great men' who possess a unique combination of traits (e.g., courage, vision, intelligence, physical ability, etc.). Over the 2,500 years that followed, the idea that leadership is the work of heroes who are born with a specific combination of qualities has been enormously influential. Even as new leadership theories developed and gained in popularity, the focus on the individual remained. For instance, contingency approaches saw leadership as the result of matching a person's personality with the right environment (Fiedler, 1964) while behavioural approaches focused on leaders' actions (Denison et al., 1995). Although transactional approaches go further in acknowledging the relationship between leaders and followers, they theorise that this centres on the exchange of favours between members of these groups (Hollander, 1978).

At this point in the book, it won't be a surprise to learn that the social identity approach considers leadership to be an outcome of group-based social processes. To illustrate this, imagine that you work as a shop assistant in a clothing store. You are paid hourly so, to earn your pay, all you *have* to do are the minimum requirements of your contract (e.g., staying for the duration of your shift, serving customers when approached, and folding clothes). As long as you fulfil these basics, how hard you work is up to you. What is it that makes you go the extra mile in this job (for instance, ensuring the shop floor is spotless or going above and beyond for a customer)? Perhaps you value hard work or customer service. Perhaps you are bored and want something to focus on. While there are several factors likely at play, the social identity approach would argue that your relationship with others in the situation (e.g., your colleagues and manager) plays a vital role in determining the effort you exert when taking part in the tasks associated with your role.

From this perspective, social influence is key to effective leadership; the most successful leaders are the ones who motivate others to believe in them (and/or the cause they represent) to such an extent that the goals of the group become synonymous with people's personal ones. In other words, people's willingness to follow a leader is contingent on how they identify with them. Going back to the example of the retail job, let's say you have a manager who spends their workday in the breakroom on social media, while you and your colleagues run the shop. How likely are you to go the extra mile for that manager? Now, let's say that instead, your manager is working alongside you, engaging in the same tasks you are (including less nice ones such as mopping the shop floor or emptying bins). How likely are you now to go the extra mile if they needed you to? Identity leadership would predict that the second manager's actions will result in the employee feeling a shared sense of identity with them; that is, their behaviours send the message that you are both working towards a common goal. As such, the employees led by this second manager may be more motivated to work hard during their shift and more committed to the company overall.

It's not just the identity you share with your manager that matters but also how you identify with your colleagues. Have you ever had a terrible manager but remained committed to your job because of the strong relationship you have with other employees? These relationships also shape your behaviour at work. Using my own academic career as an example, I might identify with my job differently depending on which part of my role is salient (e.g., as a researcher, as a teacher, as a member of my department, and as an employee of my university). How I identify with these parts of my job will be affected by my relationship with the others connected to that role (e.g., my collaborators, my students, the other psychologists in my department, and the other employees at my university). The more I perceive a shared identity with these others, the more likely I am to go the extra mile in that aspect of my role.

Given the choice, it's probably fair to assume that the senior management of my university, and the owner of the retail store used in the previous example, would opt for their staff to feel identified with their respective organizations. Indeed, organizations have a lot to benefit from having a highly identified staff, including more cooperation within the group, higher motivation, and increased productivity (Haslam, 2004). However, an identified workforce is not something that happens by accident. Rather, as a social process, it is affected by organizational systems and structures. When these highlight the identities that are shared, staff morale, and the benefits associated with this, will be boosted. However, if employees do not share an identity with others in their place of work, or worse, if they perceive other people within their organization as part of a competing out-group, then organizational functioning will be impaired (Haslam, 2004). Drawing on work that considers power as an inherent part of social relationships (Turner, 2005), this approach suggests that getting others to do a task to the best of their ability is more about increasing shared identification rather than through other means, such as coercion or by focusing on external rewards and punishments. In other words, influence happens when people feel empowered rather than forced. Hence, the social identity perspective argues that effective leadership stems from empowering people to want to do what you ask, rather than relying on the power you have over them as a means of force (Turner, 2005).

So, what is the best way to foster an identity that is strong enough that people's personal goals include advancing the group? Haslam et al. (2020) outline four elements that allow this to happen. One is that a leader should be seen as representing the group (i.e., as 'one of us'). Successful leaders emerge, or position themselves, as the group prototype (i.e., they exemplify the group's ideals; see Chapter 2). As such, when the norms and goals of the group change, so too does the group's leader. Consider the 'Partygate' scandal, where it emerged that Conservative ministers held 16 parties over the same period that the rest of the country was in lockdown to curb COVID-19 (Cabinet Office, 2022). At the time, most social gatherings had been banned, with 177,213 fixed penalty notices issued to members of the public during that time for breaking the rules set out (Maghribi, 2022). When evidence of the government's gatherings emerged, the anger from the public was palpable, with many expressing regrets at the sacrifices they had made to adhere to the rules. In this way, ministers' behaviour had undermined the feeling that everyone had been in it together. Indeed, the common trop by the media and the opposition party that there had been 'one rule for them and another rule for the rest of us.' By not following their own rules, ministers had positioned themselves as out-group and, as a result, their influence over the public waned.

A second element needed to foster identity between leaders and followers is a perception that leaders are championing the needs of the group they lead (i.e., they are *doing it for us*; Haslam et al., 2020). That is, if leaders are seen as putting their personal interests before that of the group, any influence they have over their followers will be compromised. Drawing from our discussion of the power of language to encourage (or indeed to discourage) shared identity in Chapter 6, research suggests that just using the word 'we' rather than 'I' when discussing plans for the group can encourage followers to support a leader's ideas (Steffens & Haslam, 2013). One of the most common ways that leaders tend to fail as in-group champions is by overpaying themselves. In one study, researchers presented two groups of participants with a profile of a company's Chief Executive Officer (CEO). The information given was the same except for the CEO's salary (as either moderate or high compared to others in their organization). Results showed that when participants thought that the CEO was paid in line with others (i.e., they received a moderate salary), they were rated as being more charismatic and influential. Importantly, this relationship was predicted by how identified participants felt with them (Steffens et al., 2020).

The high salaries received by senior managers can contribute to employees engaging in industrial action. In line with the idea that effective leadership requires leaders to put group interests over personal ones, a manager whose pay is viewed as extremely high compared to the pay of their employees is at risk of not only losing their influence but losing their place as a member of the group they purport to lead. This is because high pay signals that leaders are less concerned with advancing the group overall than they are with rewarding themselves as individuals. As discussed in Chapter 3, when low-status groups perceive group boundaries as impermeable (e.g., it's not possible to join the high-status out-group) and conditions as illegitimate (e.g., it's not fair that company resources are unevenly distributed), the stage is set for collective action. Over the summer of 2022, the United Kingdom has seen industrial action taking place (or being considered) by railway workers, barristers, postal workers, telecom workers, teachers, nurses, and refuse workers (among others; BBC, 2022). A key factor in all these disputes has been discontent over the distribution of pay in these sectors.

Sometimes, people emerge as leaders because of the identities they create. Haslam et al. (2020) use the term *identity entrepreneurs* to describe when leaders bring disparate individuals together under a common cause or when they are able to unite people in a new way. They point to Franklin Delano Roosevelt (FDR), the 32nd president of the United States, as embodying this concept. FDR suffered from a crippling illness (now thought to be Polio). The stigma associated with his condition should have made it impossible in 1930s America to gain support for its highest office. However, he used his illness to connect to the public, many of whom were struggling to make ends meet during the Great Depression. In this way, his condition became a metaphor for overcoming hardship, and he became the prototype of the group he led (Reicher et al., 2018). Today he is regarded as among the most important historical figures and influential U.S. presidents due to his leadership through the Great Depression and the Second World War. According to one biographer, he "lifted himself from a wheelchair to lift that nation from its knees" (Smith, 2007).

Of course, the relationship between a leader and their followers needs to be nurtured. Given the dynamic nature of group processes, a leader can only continue their influence if they work to ensure that their message remains relevant. Haslam et al. (2020) describe this element of identity leadership as 'making us matter.' Finding ways to reinforce the leaders' message in different aspects of followers' lives helps to maintain the identity they share. For instance, have you ever gone to a concert only to find yourself waiting hours for the performance to begin? Drawing on our understanding of social influence and group norms, people look to each other for guidance on how to behave. If others appear content to wait, this sends a message that the person everyone is standing around for must be worth it, increasing identity in the process. Reicher and Haslam (2017) describe Donald Trump's rallies as exemplifying this phenomenon. First, they always start late which, like with the concert example, creates a norm of devotion. Second, there tends to be a heavy security presence, sending the message that the in-group (i.e., Trump and his supporters) are under threat from an unknown out-group. As discussed in Chapter 5, intergroup threat also serves to increase in-group identification. Third, the media is required to stand in a separate space to everyone else, sometimes with a rope around them. This positioning indicates that this group must be contained and monitored, setting the foundation for Trump to discount any unflattering reporting of him or his policies. Hence, just through his rallies, Trump can embed identification with the group and cement his position as the group's leader (Reicher & Haslam, 2017).

CONCLUSION

The social identity approach to leadership brings together many of the themes and ideas presented throughout this book into an applied context that all of us, in some way or another, can relate to. However, it's far from the only one. Everywhere we look, there are examples of people interacting, whether they are working and celebrating together, engaging in the buying and selling of goods, caring for one another, or simply acknowledging each other in passing. Hence, everywhere we look, there are examples of social influence of people following along with others. As we've explored in this book, any interaction is intergroup as much as it is interpersonal. It is the nature of these relationships, in terms of how much we identify with these others, that play a key role in determining who we are. In other words, our self is tied to our identities.

CHAPTER SUMMARY

- Leadership is not about individual traits or behaviours but an outcome of group processes.
- Influence over others is a function of how identified followers are with a leader and the cause that leader represents.
- There are four elements that facilitate identity-based leadership: being seen as one of the group, as working for the group's best interests, as making the group matter in a broader context, and as maintaining the shared identity that holds the group together.

WANT TO KNOW MORE?

Recommended Reading:
*   Haslam, S. A., Reicher, S. D., & Platow, M. J. (2020). *The new psychology of leadership: Identity, influence and power*. Routledge

REFERENCES

BBC. (2022, September 29). Who's going on strike and when? *British Broadcasting Company* https://www.bbc.co.uk/news/uk-62632167

Cabinet Office. (2022, May 25). Findings of second permanent secretary's investigation into alleged gatherings on government premises during covid restrictions. https://assets.publishing.service.gov.uk/government/uploads/system/uploads/attachment_data/file/1078404/2022-05-25_FINAL_FINDINGS_OF_SECOND_PERMANENT_SECRETARY_INTO_ALLEGED_GATHERINGS.pdf

Denison, D., Hooijberg, R., & Quinn, R. E. (1995). Paradox and performance: Toward a theory of behavioral complexity in managerial leadership. *Organization Science, 6*, 524–540. https://doi.org/10.1287/orsc.6.5.524

Fiedler, F. E. (1964). A contingency model of leadership effectiveness. In L. Berkowitz (Ed.), *Advances in experimental social psychology* (Vol. 1, pp. 149–190). Academic Press https://doi.org/10.1016/S0065-2601(08)60051-9

Haslam, S. A. (2004). *Psychology in organizations*. Sage

Haslam, S. A., Reicher, S. D., & Platow, M. J. (2020). *The new psychology of leadership: Identity, influence and power*. Routledge

Hollander, E. E. (1978). *Leadership dynamics: A practical guide to effective relationships*. Free Press/Macmillan

Maghribi, L. (2022). Downing street scandal: Pardons and refunds sought for thousands fined over Covid breaches. https://www.thenationalnews.com/world/uk-news/2022/01/13/downing-street

Reicher, S., & Haslam, S. A. (2017). The politics of hope: Donald Trump as an entrepreneur of identity. In M. Fitzduff (Ed.), *Why irrational politics appeals: Understanding the allure of Trump* (pp. 25–40). Praeger

Reicher, S. D., Haslam, S. A., & Platow, M. J. (2018). Shared social identity in leadership. *Current Opinion in Psychology, 23*, 129–133. https://doi.org/10.1016/j.copsyc.2018.08.006

Smith, J. E. (2007). *FDR*. Random House

Steffens, N. K., & Haslam, S. A. (2013). Power through 'us': Leaders' use of we-referencing language predicts election victory. *PLoS One, 8*(10), e77952.

Steffens, N. K., Haslam, S. A., Peters, K., & Quiggin, J. (2020). Identity econom-
ics meets identity leadership: Exploring the consequences of elevated CEO
pay. *The Leadership Quarterly, 31*(3), 101269. https://doi.org/10.1016/j.
leaqua.2018.10.001

Turner, J. C. (2005). Explaining the nature of power: A three-process theory.
European Journal of Social Psychology, 35(1), 1–22. https://doi.org/10.1002/
ejsp.244

GLOSSARY

Accent
Any speech pattern that is more or less similar to the standard within a population

Agentic traits
Traits often associated with men (e.g., ambition, assertiveness, dominance)

Ambivalent sexism theory
A theoretical framework which suggests that sexism has two sub-components: hostile sexism and benevolent sexism

Attribution errors
Mistakes made when interpreting the causes for a specific event of behaviour

Audience tuning
Adjusting how one communicates based on their communication partner

Benevolent sexism
A form of paternalistic prejudice, a patronising yet affectionate view of women

Collectivist cultures
Cultures which emphasise the needs and goals of the group as a whole rather than the desires and needs of each individual

Common bond group
An affiliation based on an attachment between group members

Common identity group
An affiliation based on a shared connection to an overarching category

Communal traits
Traits often associated with women (e.g., warm, compassionate, emotional)

Contact quality
Deep positive and personal relationships with out-group members

Contact quantity
The frequency of interactions with out-group members

Convergence
Adapting our communication towards that of our communication partner

Cooperation
The process of working with others in order to reach the same goal

Demographic vitality
The number of speakers within a linguistic community

Depersonalisation
A state in which your feelings and thoughts seem unreal or like they belong to someone else

Diffusion of responsibility
When the number of people present results in less people taking responsibility

Divergence
Adapting our communication away from that of our partner

Downward comparisons
Judging yourself against people who are less skilled and/or fortunate than you

Dualism
The notion that humans consist of body and soul, and that the two are separate from one another

Efficacy-based self-esteem
The extent that we see ourselves as capable

Ethnolinguistic identity
Feeling of belonging based on a common ancestry and language

Ethnolinguistic vitality
The status of one's language

Event schemas
Knowledge about how to behave in the immediate social environment

Explicit norms
Stated clearly rules of behaviour

Extended contact
An awareness of in-group members having relationships with out-group members

False consensus effect
A type of bias in which an individual thinks that their own opinions and attitudes are more common than they really are

Genocide
The deliberate killing of a large number of people from a particular nation or group with the intent of destroying that nation or group

Group polarisation
The tendency for a group to make decisions that are more extreme than the initial beliefs of its members

Hostile sexism
Predicts negative evaluations of women who violate traditional gender stereotypes

Imagined contact
Envisioning an interaction with an out-group member

Implicit norms
Unspoken and assumed rules of behaviour

Impression management
The process in which people attempt to control how others perceive them

Individualistic cultures
Cultures which emphasise skills such as independency, autonomy, and self-expression. Individual goals are perceived as more important than the group as a whole

Informational influence
Conforming because of the belief that others are correct

Ingratiation
The act of showing qualities to make a person think positively of you

Institutional support
Support of the use of a language in public places

Intergroup relations
The interactions between individuals in different social groups

Intimidation
To frighten or deter others

Looseness–tightness dimension
How strictly social norms are expected to be followed and the degree of sanctions imposed on those who do not adhere to these norms

Marginal group members
In-group members that are considered deviant

Non-verbal communication
The behavioural elements of communication

Normative influence
Conforming in order to be accepted by others

Norms
Group rules for behaviour

Ostracism
Exclusion from a society or group

Person schemas
Knowledge about specific people

Personal identity
The attributes that make you an individual

Power distance
The degree to which less powerful members of institutions and organizations accept that power is distributed unequally.

Prejudice
A negative feeling about a person that is based on their social group

Private self-awareness
How we feel and think about our self

Privileged
Special rights, advantages, and/or immunities because of one's group membership

Prototype
A group member who embodies all of the traits important to that group

Public self-awareness
The belief we have about how others see us

Reincarnation
The belief that after death, a being's spirit inhabits another body

Relational self-construal
Defining oneself based on the closeness of their relationships with others

Role schemas
Knowledge about what is appropriate based on people's position in a group

Salience
When something is particularly noticeable or prominent

Saying is believing effect
A phenomenon where what we say is consistent with what we've actually said, rather than our original belief

Schema
A cognitive structure representing our understanding of a concept or social stimulus

Schism
A division between strongly opposed groups due to differences in opinions and/or beliefs

Self-awareness
The attention that we devote to our self

Self-concept
What we think about who we are

Self-construal
The cognitive representation individuals hold of their self

Self-esteem
Our evaluation of ourselves as positive or negative

Self-promotion
The action of promoting yourself or your activities

Self-regulation
The ability to regulate yourself without an intervention from external factors

Self-schemas
The specific knowledge we have out our self

Shared reality
The feeling of sharing a common experience with someone else

Social cognition
The mental activity responsible for processing social information

Social group
Two or more people who interact with one another, share characteristics, and have a sense of unity

Social reflection
How the media directly reflects and impacts the values, norms, and beliefs of our culture

Social role
The part that you play as a member of a social group

Status vitality
A language's prestige

Stereotype content model
The idea that our judgement of others is based on our perception of them as warm and competent

Stereotype threat
A phenomenon where an individual fears confirming stereotypes about their social group, and this interferes with their ability to perform in an identity relevant task

Stereotypes
A widely held but fixed and oversimplified idea of a person based on their social categories

Stigma
An attribute that discredits an individual by marking them in a way that reduces their value to others in a social group

Tokenism
A positive but trivial act to benefit a minority group

Uncertainty avoidance
The extent to which ambiguity in society is limited through tradition and religion

Upward comparisons
When you compare yourself to someone, you perceive to be superior to yourself

Verbal communication
Spoken language that sends an intentional message to the listener

Vicarious contact
Observing how an in-group members interacts with an out-group member

Virtual contact
Contact with an out-group member over a computer

Visual communication
The transmission of ideas through symbols and imagery

Worth-based self-esteem
How valued and accepted we feel by others

INDEX

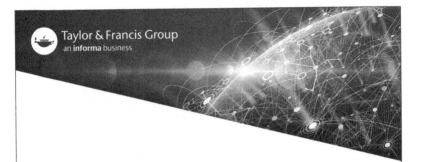

reinforces how Sophie sees Mary but can influence our own ideas about Mary (even if we choose the word based on what we think Sophie's perception of Mary is, rather than our own opinions of Mary!). According to the 'saying is belief effect,' what we remember tends to be consistent with what we've said, even if what we've said was based on our ideas about others' beliefs (Higgins & Rholes, 1978). In other words, we remember the message of the words we tuned, rather than any original opinions we had. However, this recall bias is not automatic; for our memories of the target to be influenced by our use of audience tuning, we must trust our communication partner (Echterhoff et al., 2008) and feel that we've been successful in creating a shared sense of reality with them (Pinelli et al., 2022).

Accommodating our messages also allows us to manage our own identity. How this happens can be understood through *communication accommodation theory* (i.e., CAT; Giles, 2016). According to this theory, there are two main ways that we adjust (or accommodate) how we communicate. The one we choose depends on how we position our identity to that of the person we are interacting with. If we think of our communication partner as an in-group member, we're likely to engage in *convergence* where we adapt our language towards that of our partner. If we think of our communication partner as a member of an out-group, we'll engage in *divergence* where we emphasise differences in our way of speaking, allowing us to distance ourselves from our partner. While we have been focusing specifically on spoken language throughout this chapter, CAT considers all types of communication (e.g., amount of eye contact, etc.) as able to be accommodated. Exactly how that communication adapted depends on both identity processes and the goal we have the exchange.

To illustrate this, let's use the following example: A professor wants to motivate a student might align their language to that of the student's (e.g., by speaking casually, asking the student to call them by their first name, or imitating phrases that students tend to use). In this way, the professor uses language to position themselves as a member of the student's in-group, which sends the message to the student that they are working towards the same goal. However, the professor may also decide to position themselves as out-group to the student, perhaps because they want to assert their authority

Higgins (1992) calls this phenomenon *audience tuning* or, using the language that most closely aligns with the beliefs of your listener. To some extent, we do this in every communication exchange. For instance, we often use a different language to communicate with our family than we do with our work colleagues. Certain environments also encourage specific ways of speaking; while an office setting might call for formal language, a pub is generally a place where we speak more causally. Most of us will also recognise differences in how we speak to friends versus authority figures, or that words come more easily when conversing with people we know well as opposed to when interacting with strangers. Varying one's language based on the characteristics of the listener, or to suit a particular environment, is something we often do without thinking much about it (Higgins, 1981).

How we modify our language depends on several factors. Some examples include the goal we have for the exchange (e.g., to provide customer service, to make someone laugh; Echterhoff et al., 2008) or the status differences that exist between ourselves and our communication partner (e.g., an interviewee is more likely to tune their language towards that of the hiring manager than the other way around; Gregory & Webster, 1996). Yet, whatever the reason, the success of any communication exchange depends on our ability to create a shared reality between ourselves and the person we are communicating with (Higgins et al., 2021). A *shared reality* describes the feeling of sharing a common experience with someone else (see Echterhoff & Higgins, 2018). Our ability to connect with others b[y] matching language and following shared social norms about how [we] use language helps to both deepen our relationships and understa[nd] what is happening around us. Hence, the shared reality that is c[re]ated through language draws on two key ideas we have discusse[d] this book so far. First, it allows us to fulfil our fundamental psyc[ho]logical need to connect with other human beings (see Chapter[).] Second, it validates our experiences, something that we depend o[n] others to do (see Chapter 4).

However, the shared reality we create through language has implications for the way we perceive ourselves and others. Let's think back to the example above where we tuned our message about Mary's lack of spending in line with our perception of Sophie's attitudes about Mary. The connotations attached to the word we use not only